FOR ORGANS, PIANOS & ELECTRONIC KEYBOARDS

E-Z PLAY TODAY

16

BROADWAY'S BEST
3RD EDITION

ISBN 978-1-5400-2271-4

HAL•LEONARD®
7777 W. BLUEMOUND RD. P.O. BOX 13819 MILWAUKEE, WI 53213

Visit Hal Leonard Online at
www.halleonard.com

Bali Ha'i
from SOUTH PACIFIC

Registration 5
Rhythm: Fox Trot

Lyrics by Oscar Hammerstein II
Music by Richard Rodgers

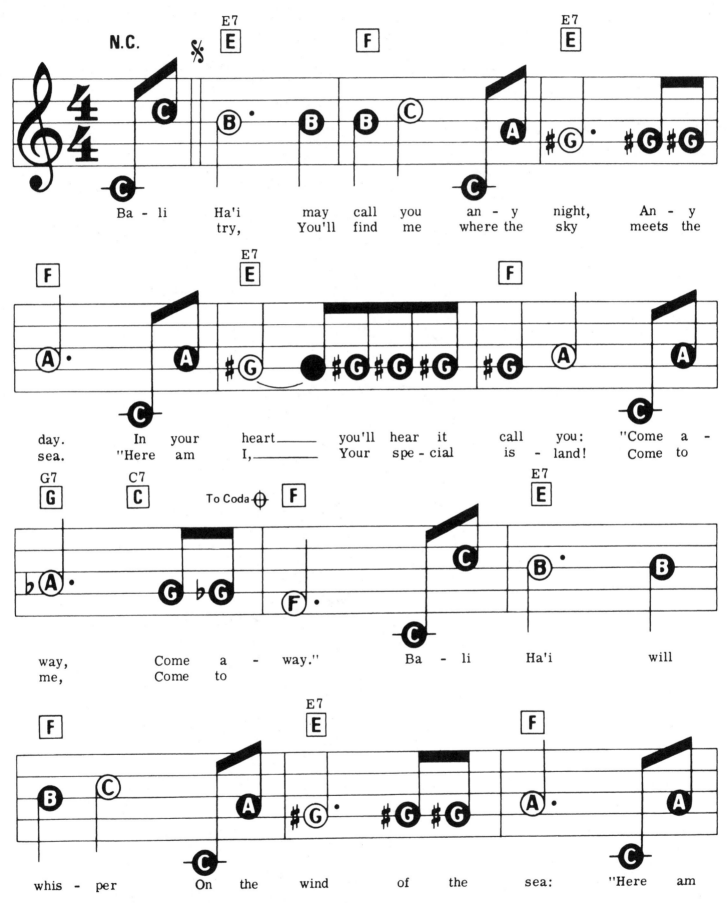

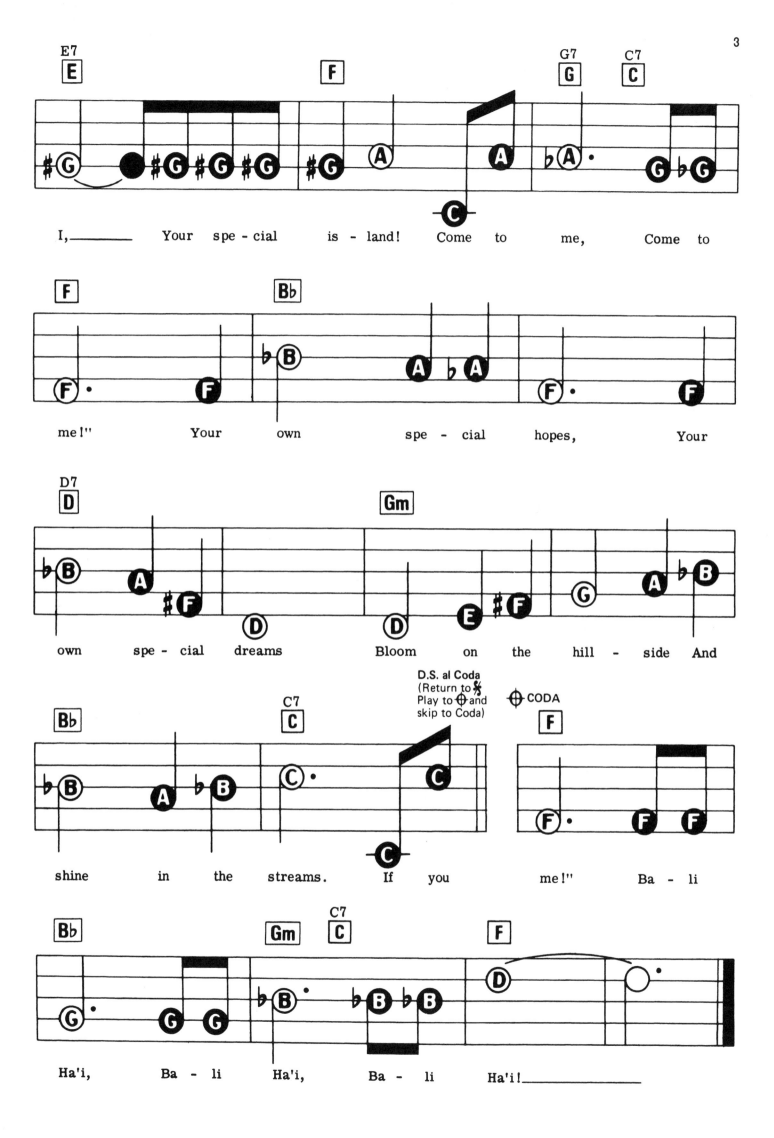

Cabaret
from the Musical CABARET

Registration 7
Rhythm: Swing

Words by Fred Ebb
Music by John Kander

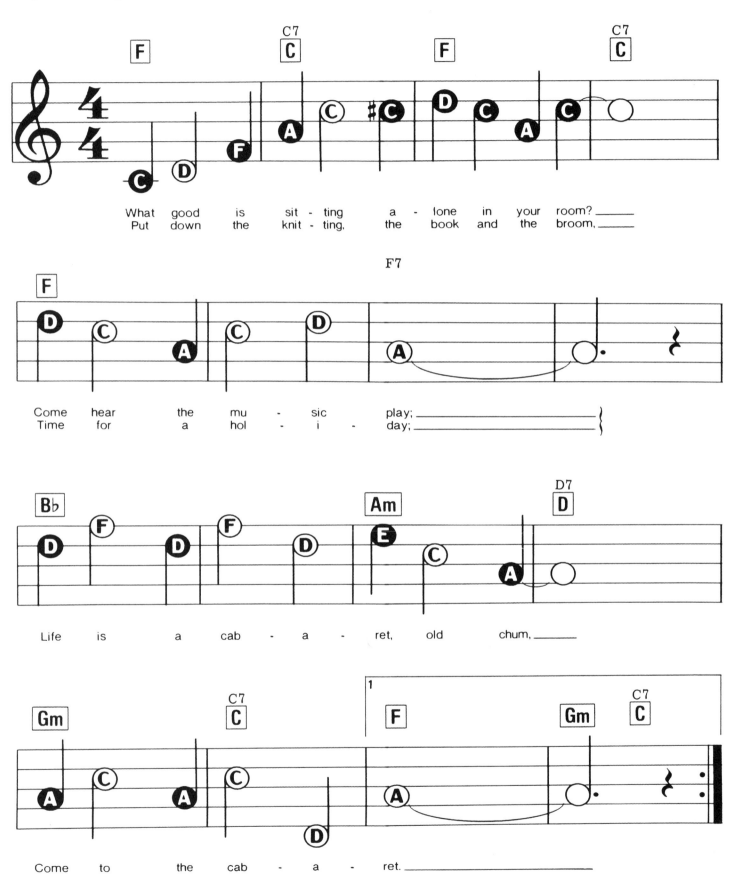

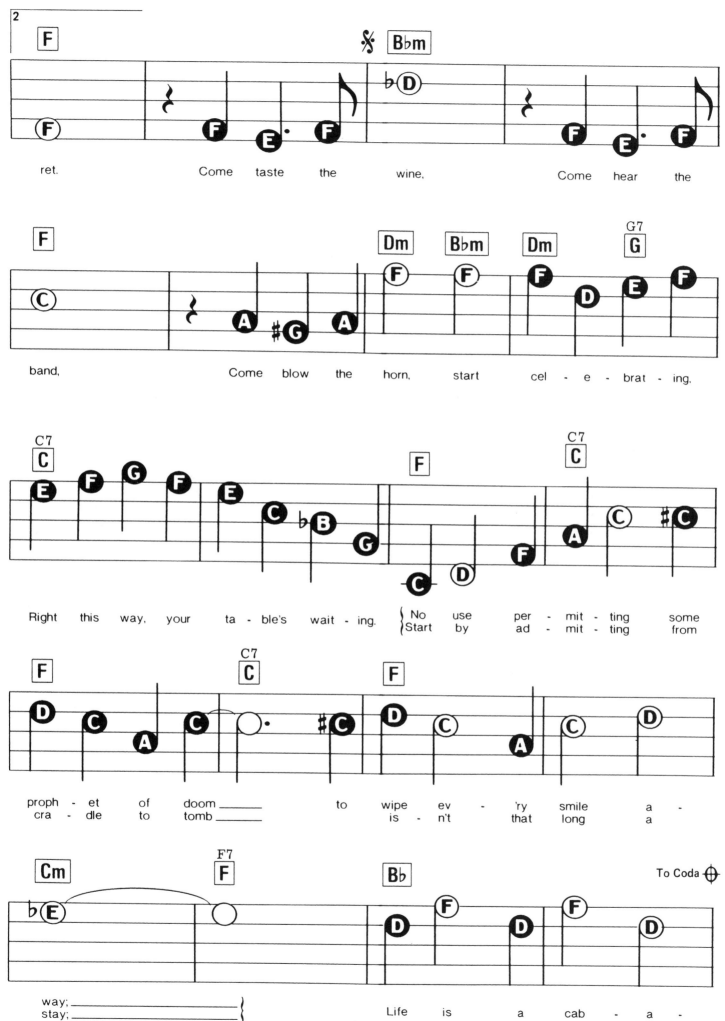

6

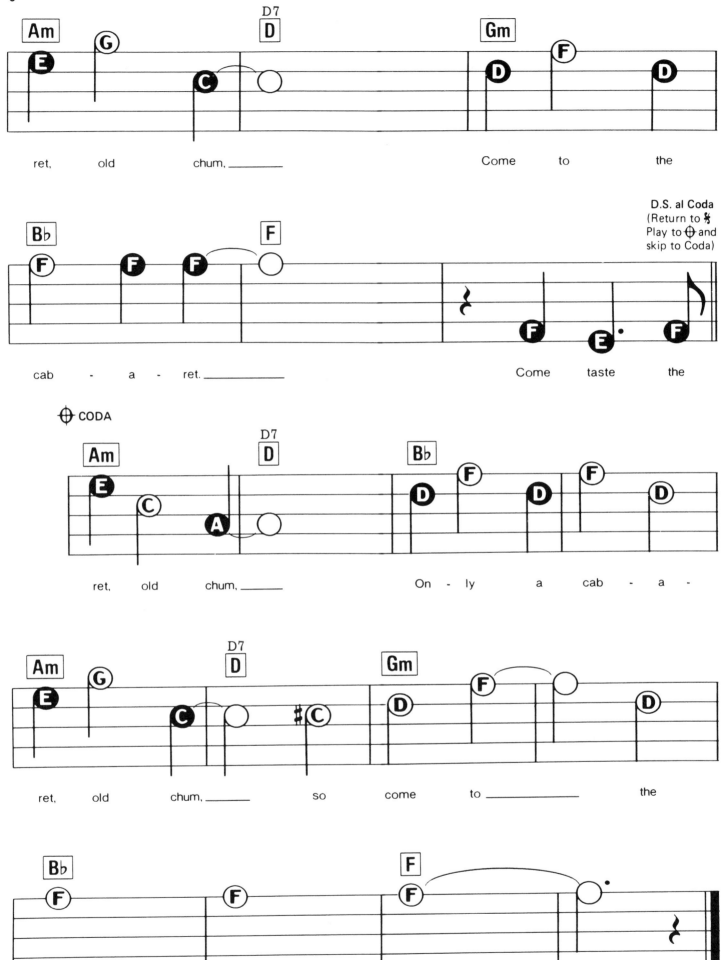

Defying Gravity
from the Broadway Musical WICKED

Registration 7
Rhythm: Pop or Rock

Music and Lyrics by
Stephen Schwartz

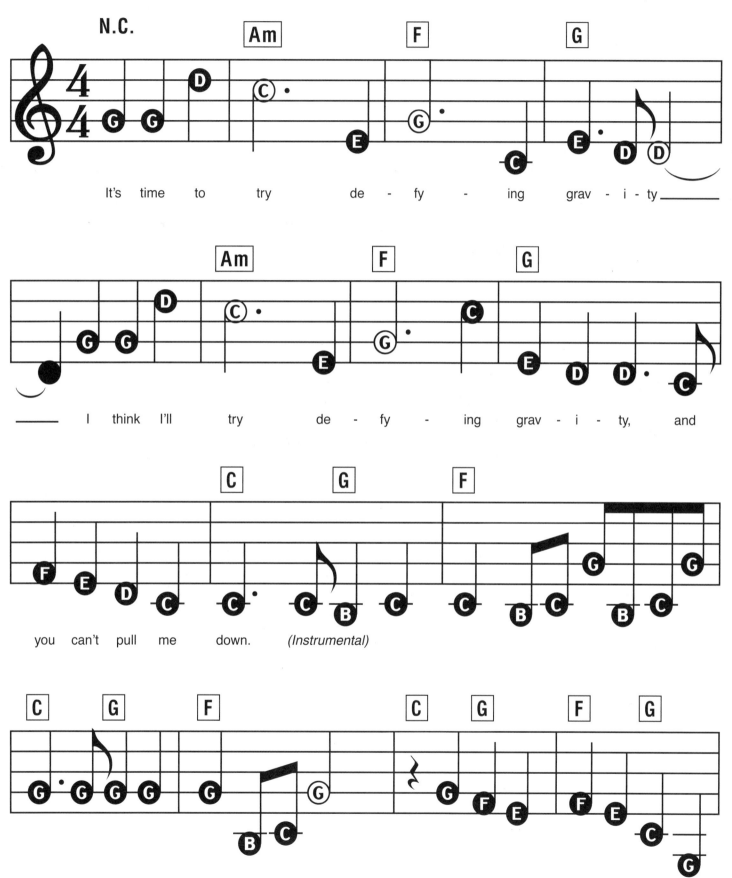

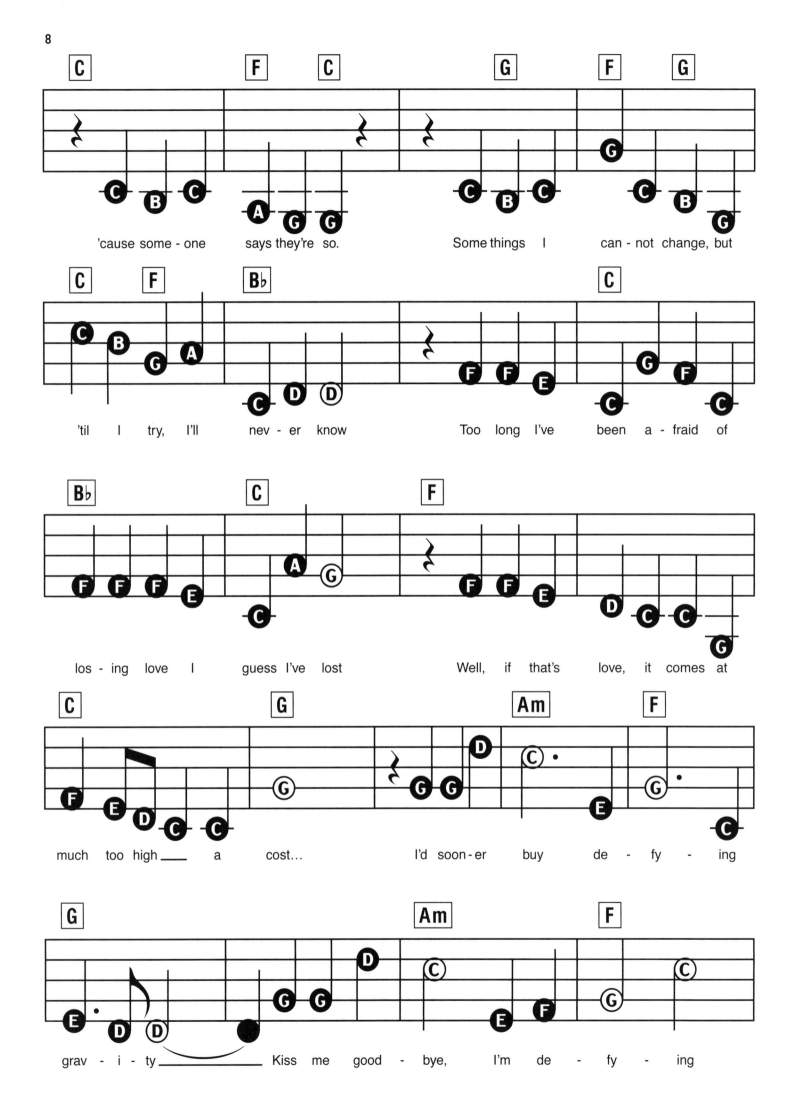

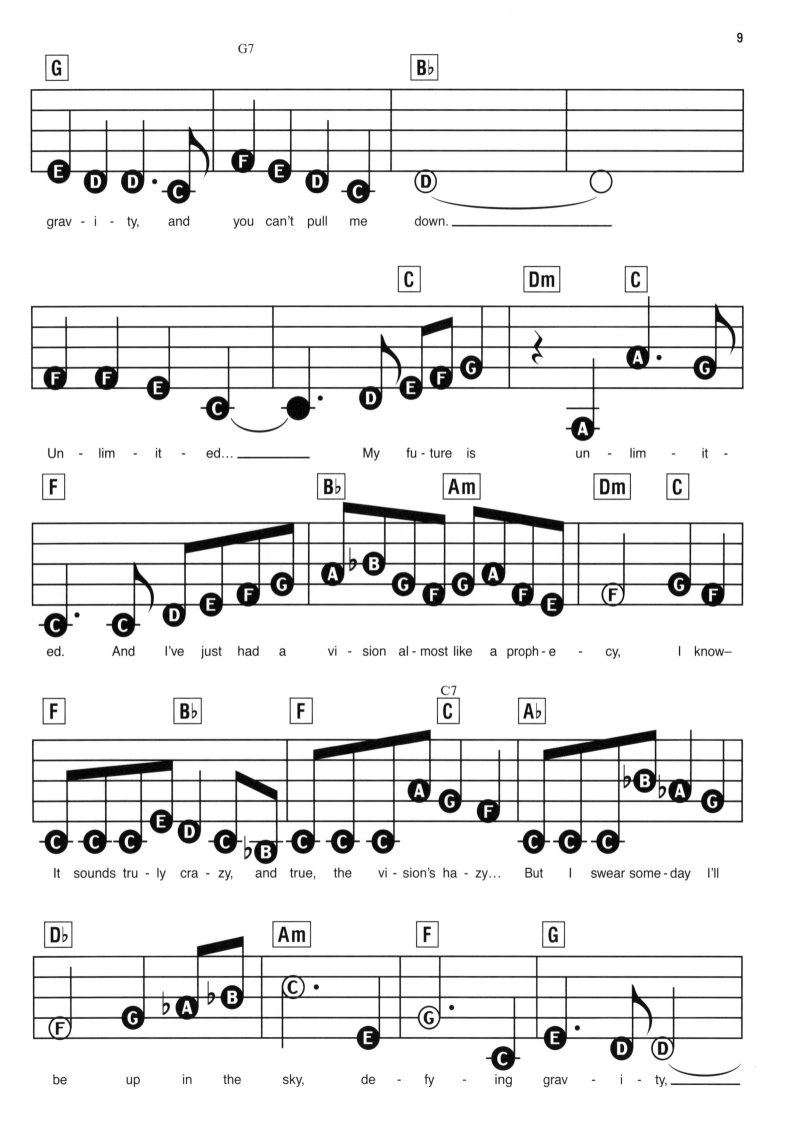

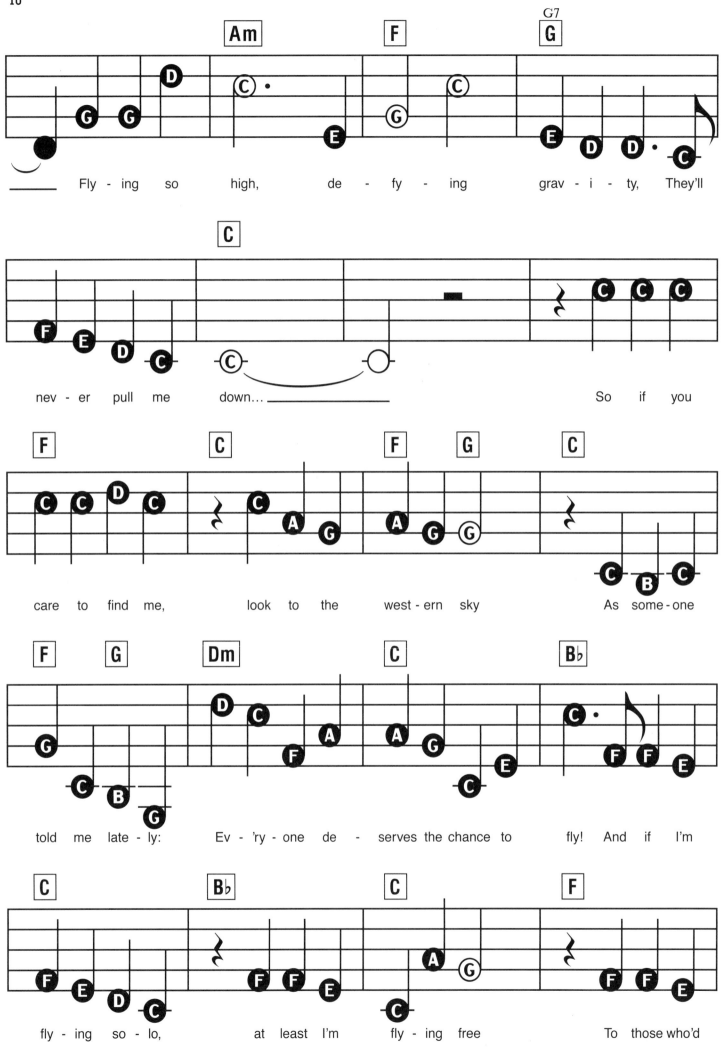

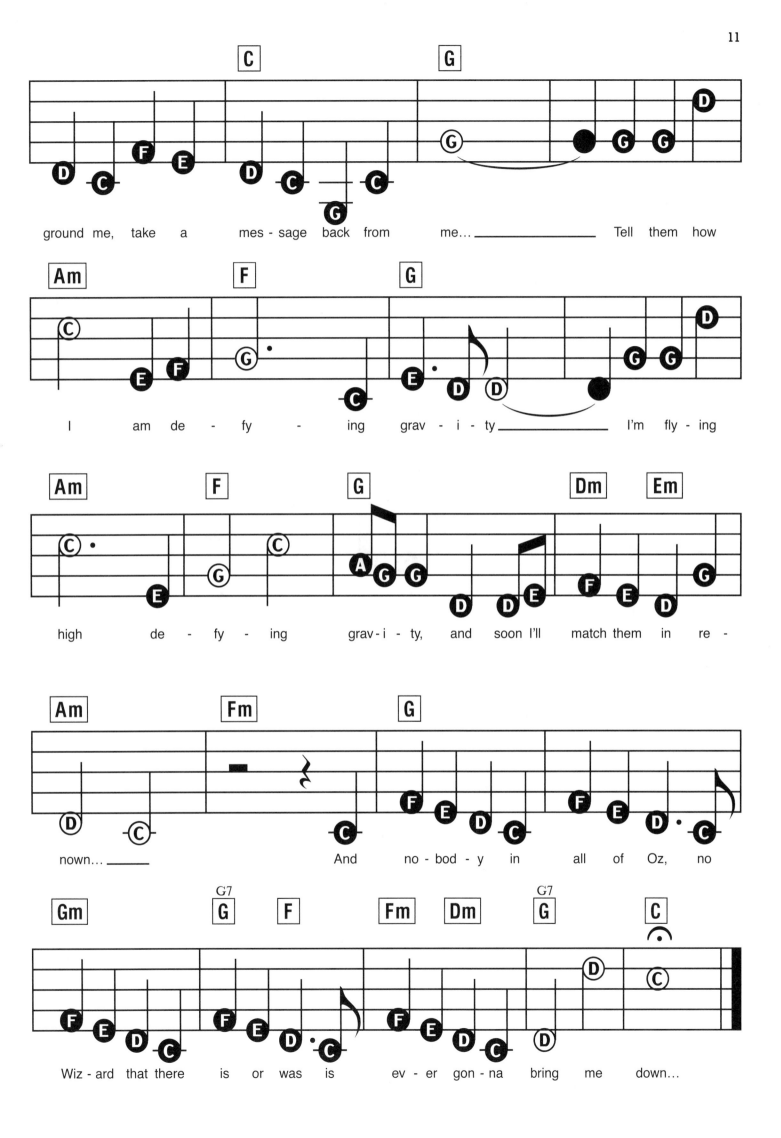

Can't Help Lovin' Dat Man
from SHOW BOAT

Registration 5
Rhythm: Ballad or Swing

Lyrics by Oscar Hammerstein II
Music by Jerome Kern

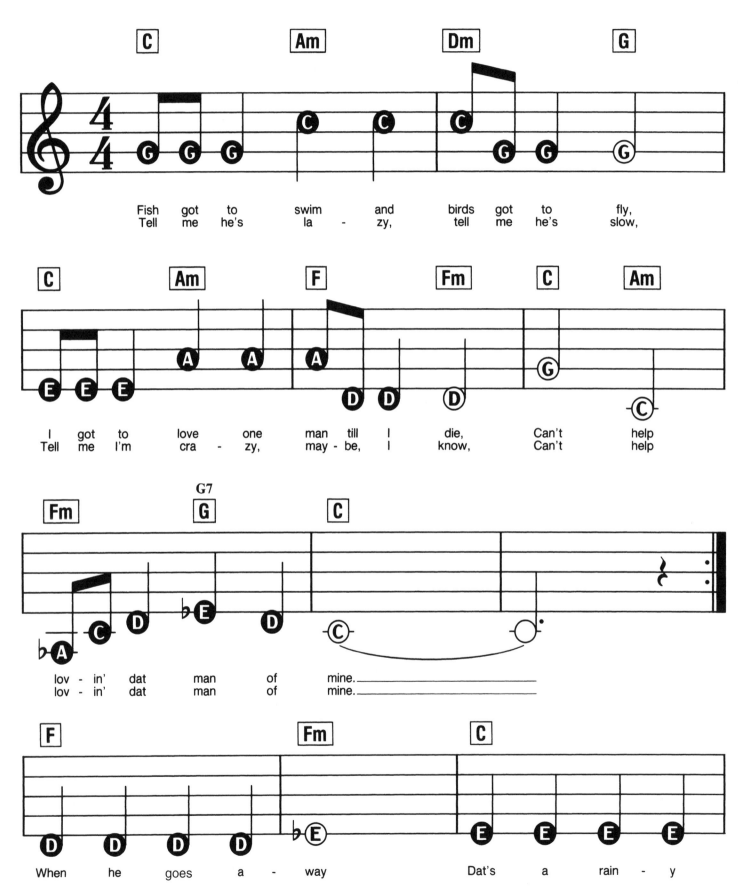

Climb Ev'ry Mountain
from THE SOUND OF MUSIC

Registration 5
Rhythm: Ballad

Lyrics by Oscar Hammerstein II
Music by Richard Rodgers

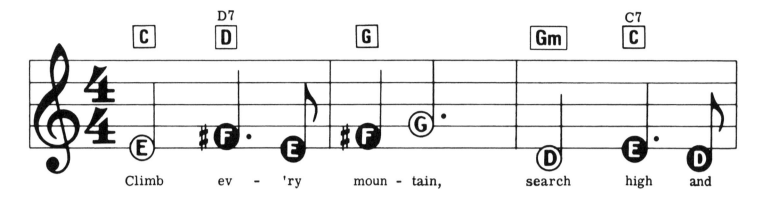

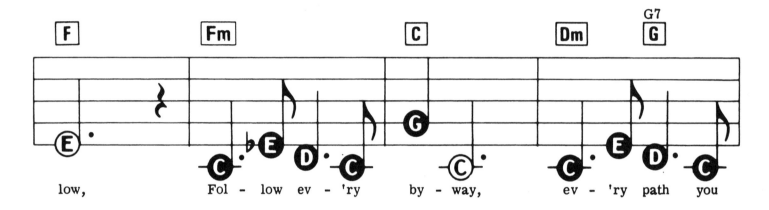

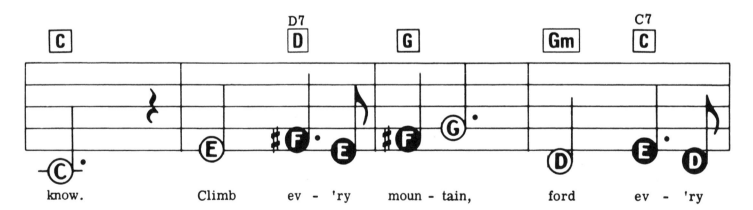

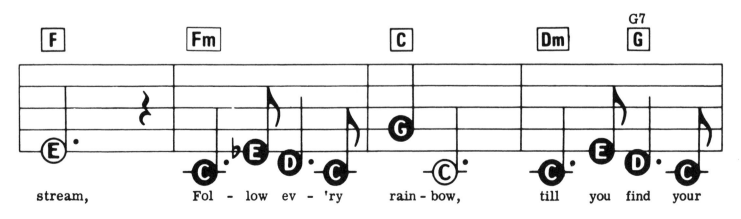

Dear Theodosia
from HAMILTON

Registration 8
Rhythm: Ballad or None

Words and Music by
Lin-Manuel Miranda

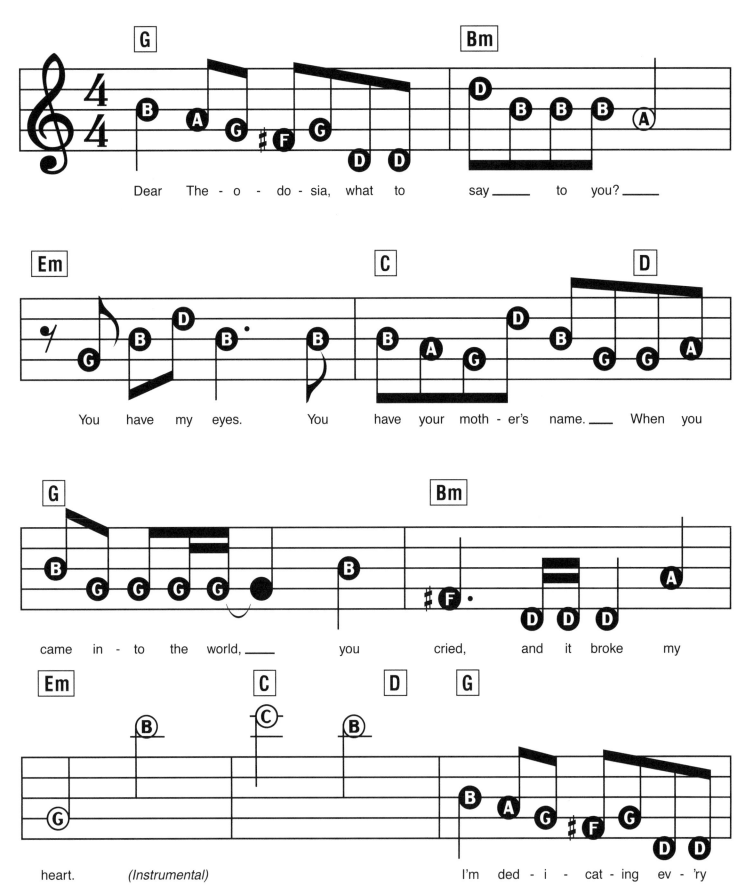

17

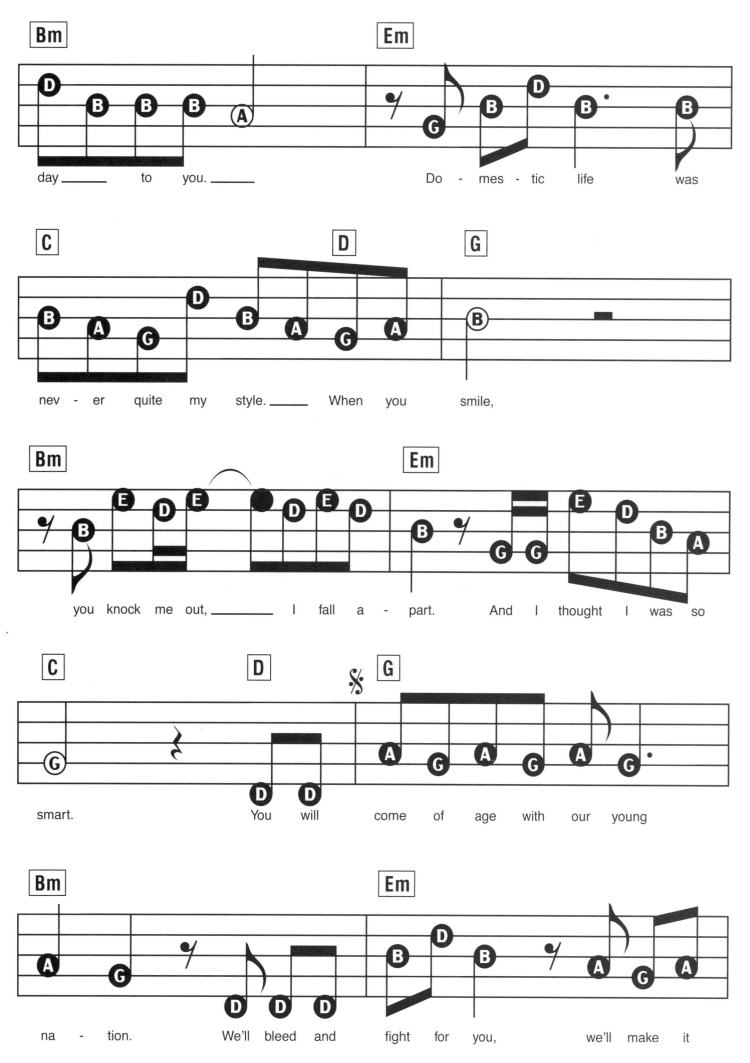

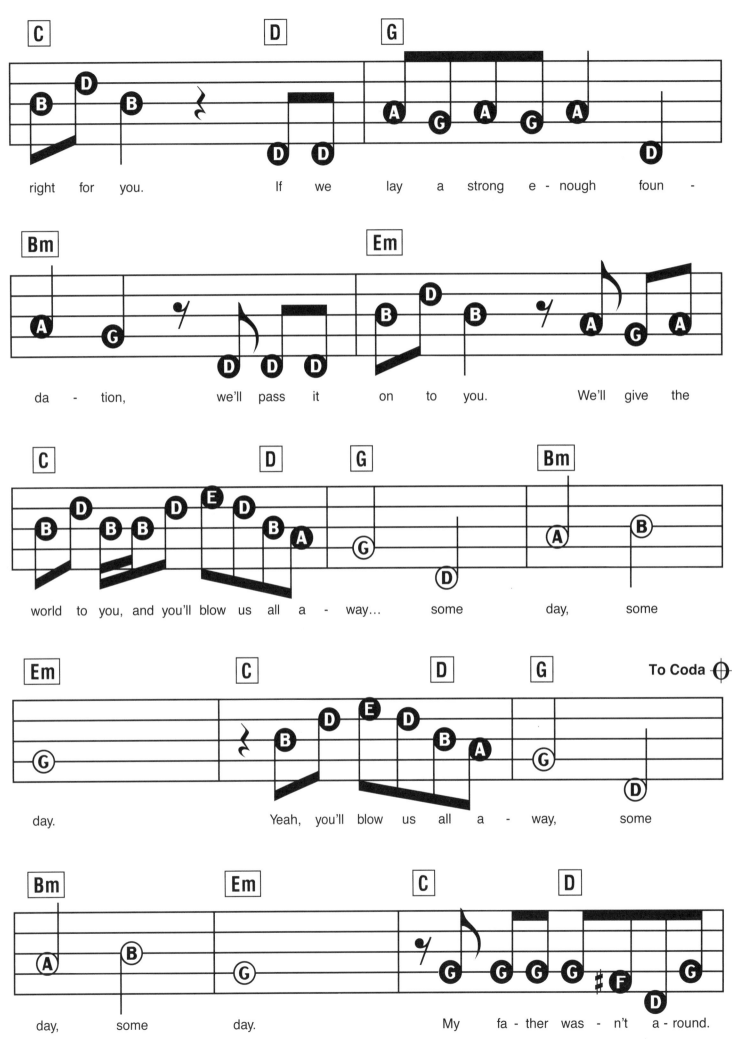

19

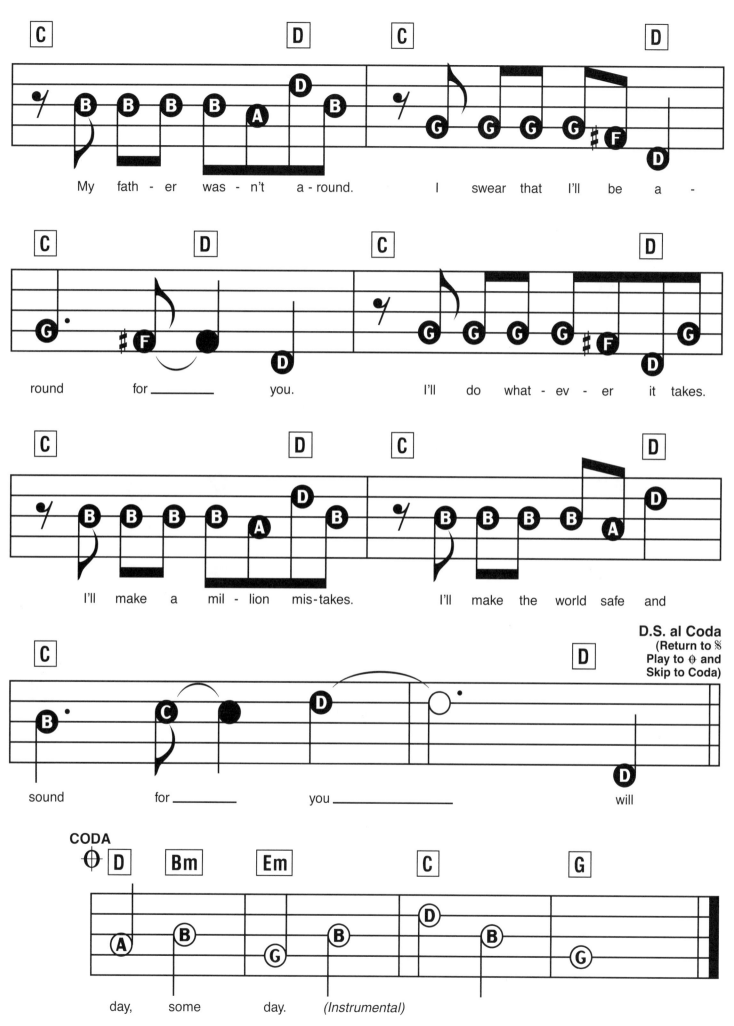

Do-Re-Mi
from THE SOUND OF MUSIC

Registration 4
Rhythm: Fox Trot or March

Lyrics by Oscar Hammerstein II
Music by Richard Rodgers

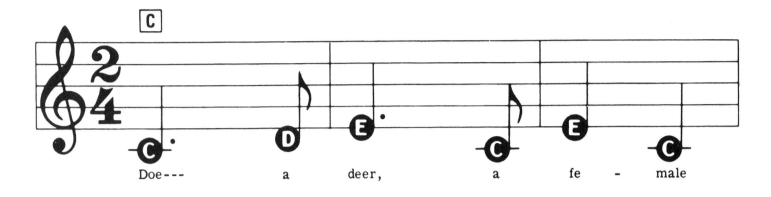

Doe--- a deer, a fe - male

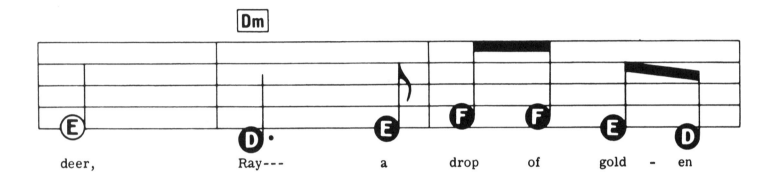

deer, Ray--- a drop of gold - en

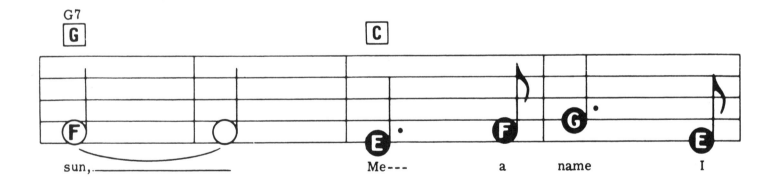

sun,_____ Me--- a name I

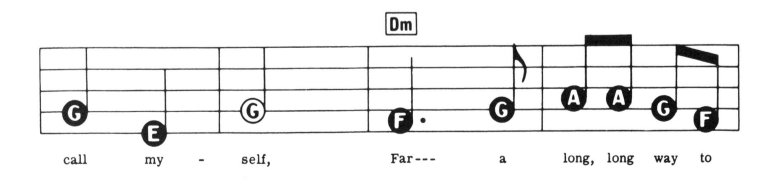

call my - self, Far--- a long, long way to

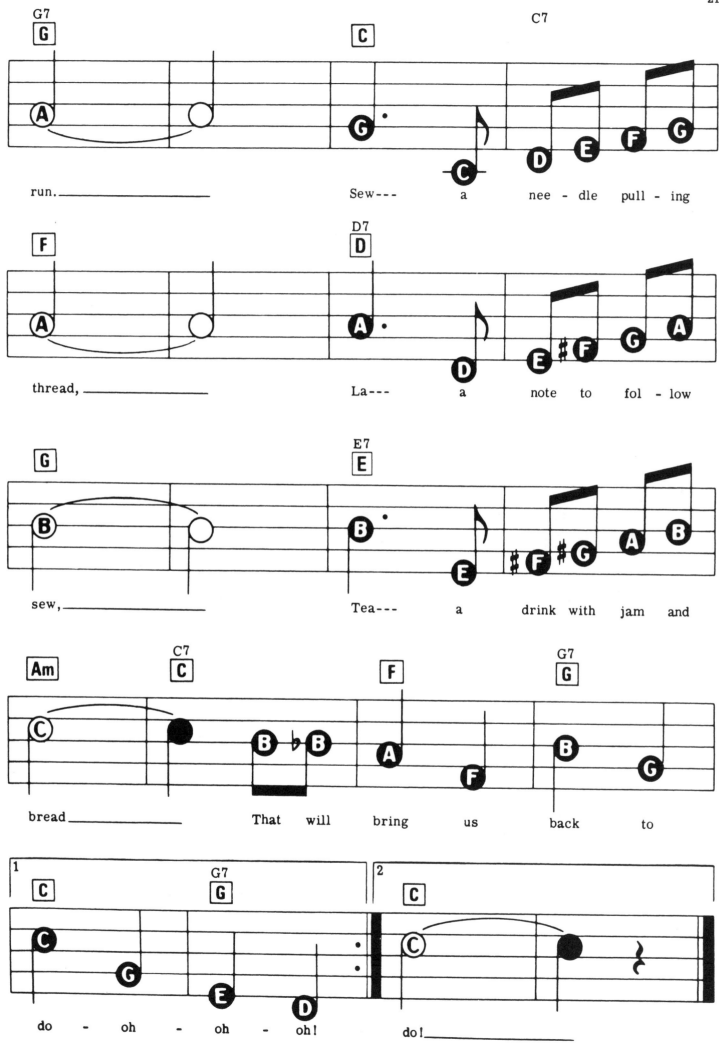

Edelweiss
from THE SOUND OF MUSIC

Registration 4
Rhythm: Waltz

Lyrics by Oscar Hammerstein II
Music by Richard Rodgers

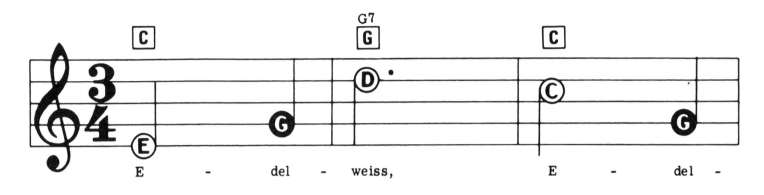

E - del - weiss,   E - del -

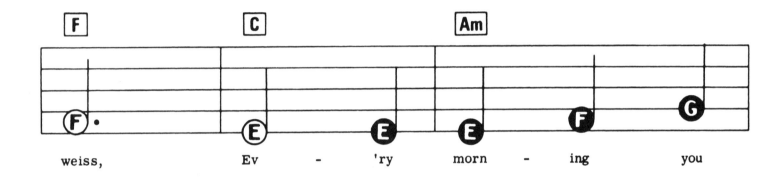

weiss,   Ev - 'ry morn - ing you

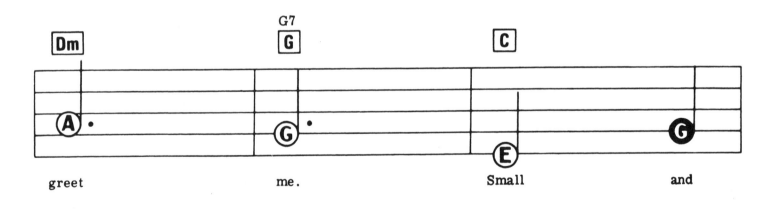

greet   me.   Small   and

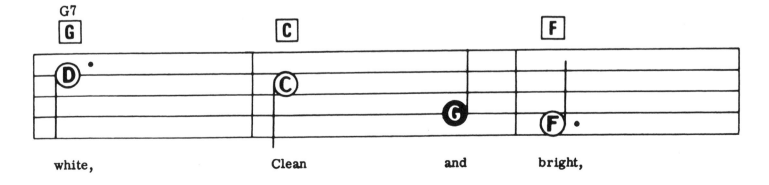

white,   Clean and bright,

23

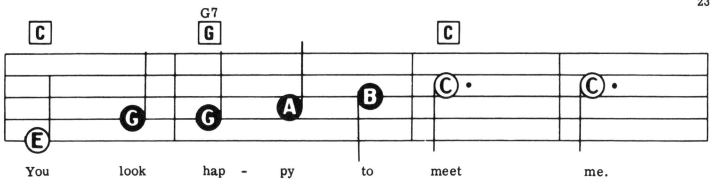

You look hap - py to meet me.

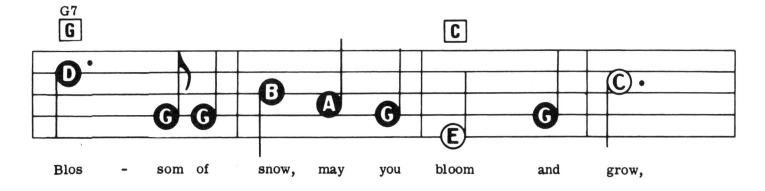

Blos - som of snow, may you bloom and grow,

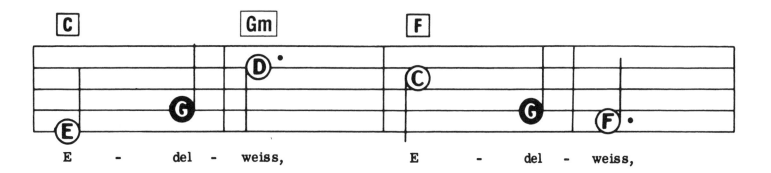

Bloom and grow for - ev - er.

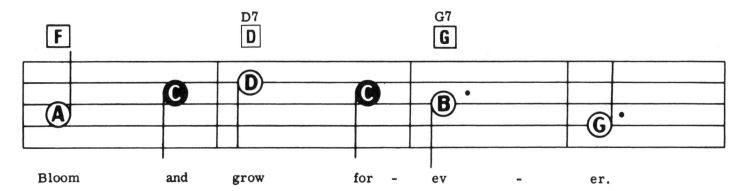

E - del - weiss, E - del - weiss,

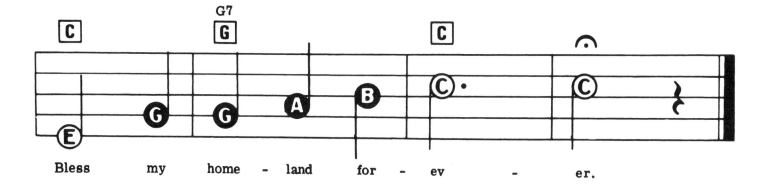

Bless my home - land for - ev - er.

Finishing the Hat
from SUNDAY IN THE PARK WITH GEORGE

Registration 2
Rhythm: None

Words and Music by
Stephen Sondheim

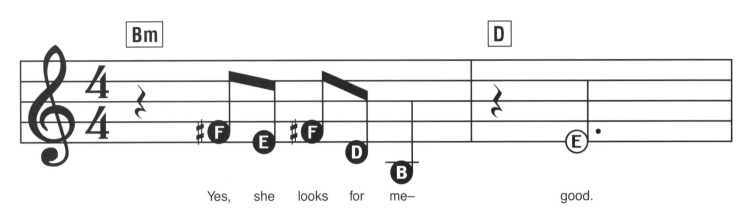

Yes, she looks for me— good.

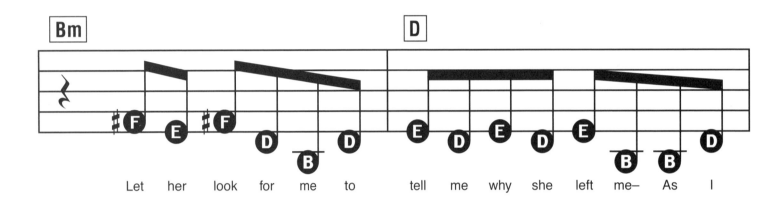

Let her look for me to tell me why she left me— As I

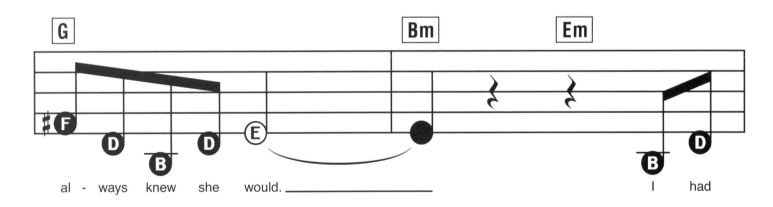

al - ways knew she would. _____ I had

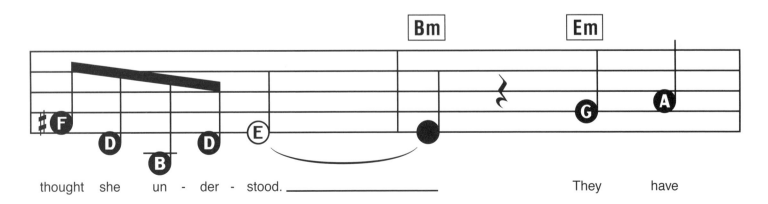

thought she un - der - stood. _____ They have

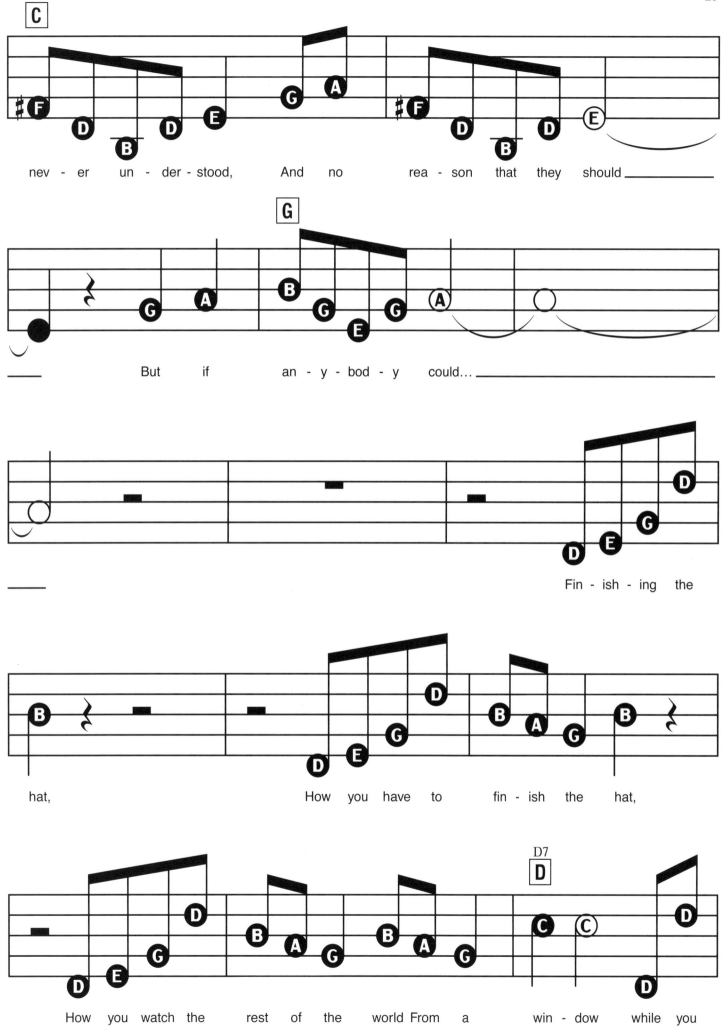

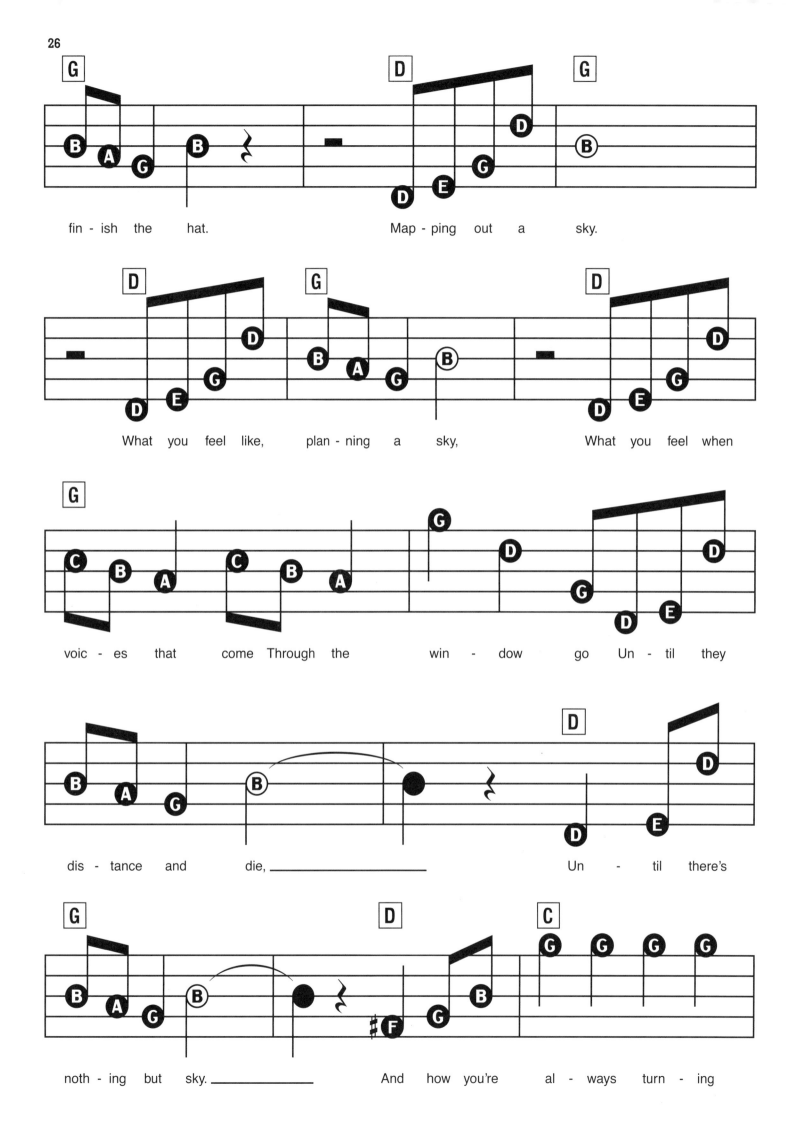

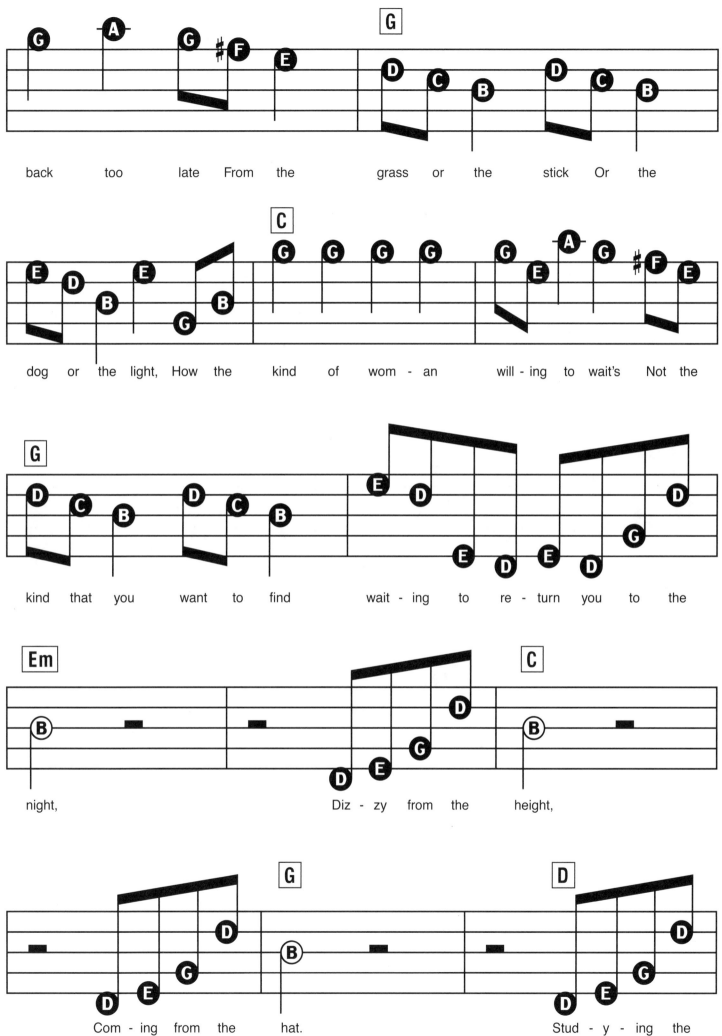

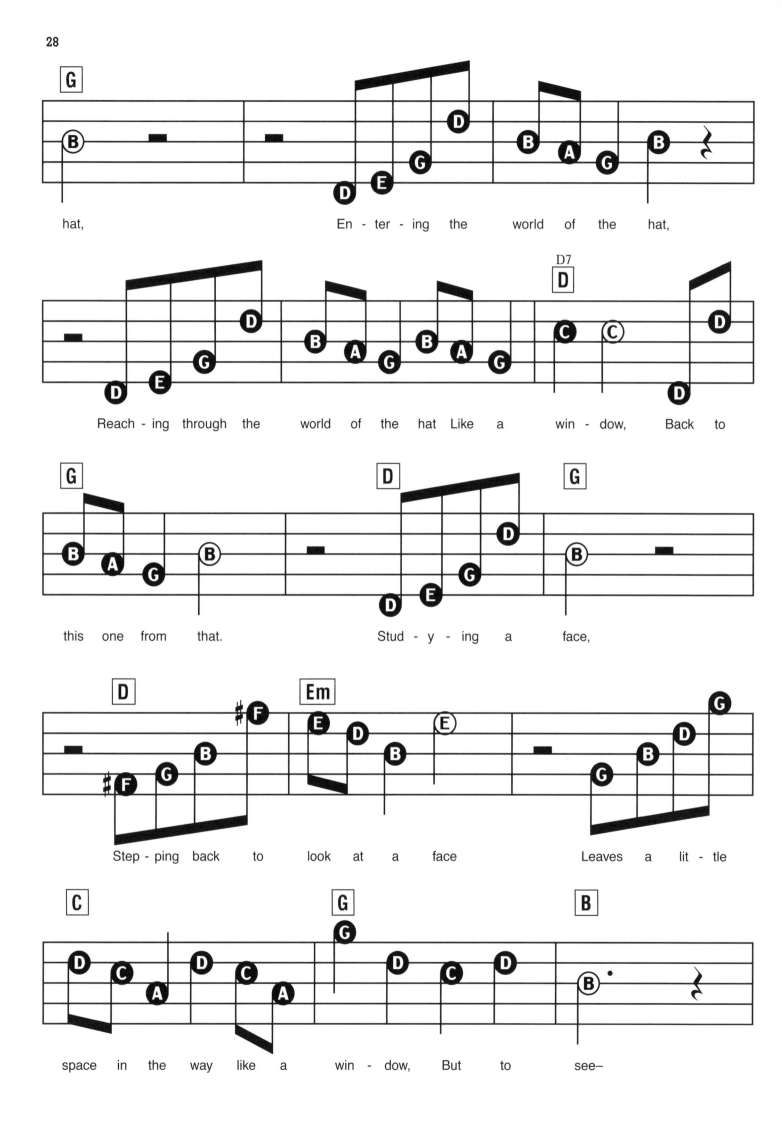

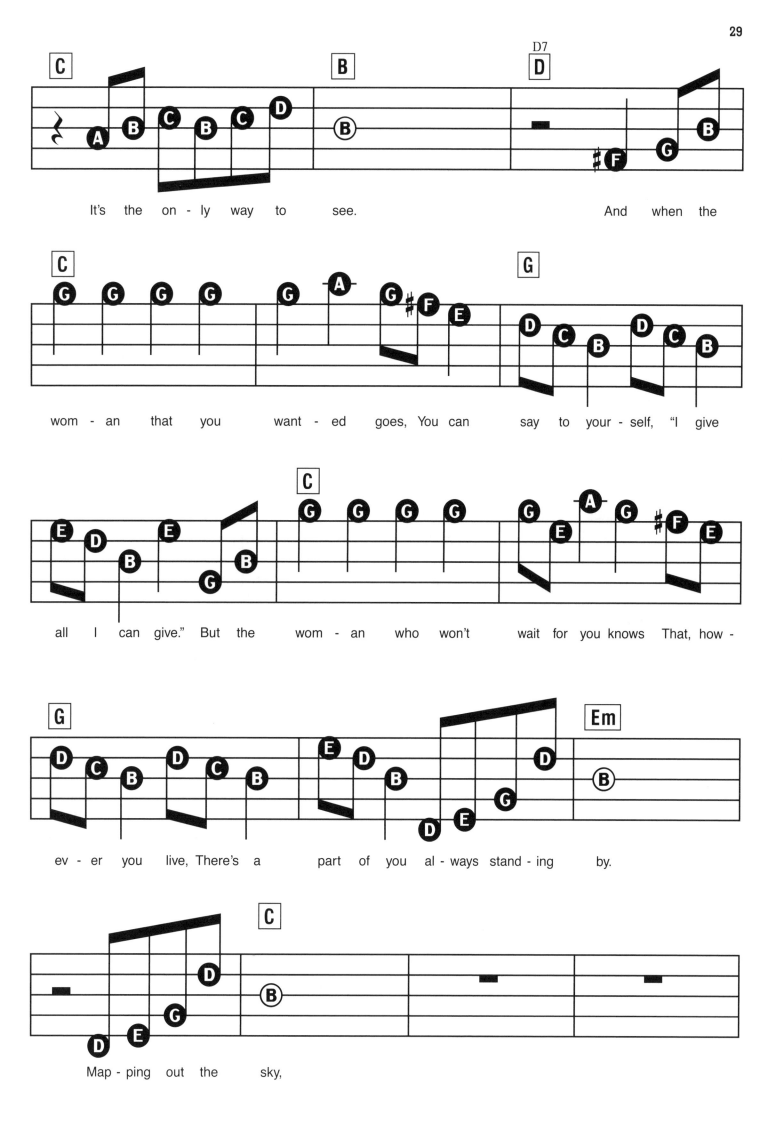

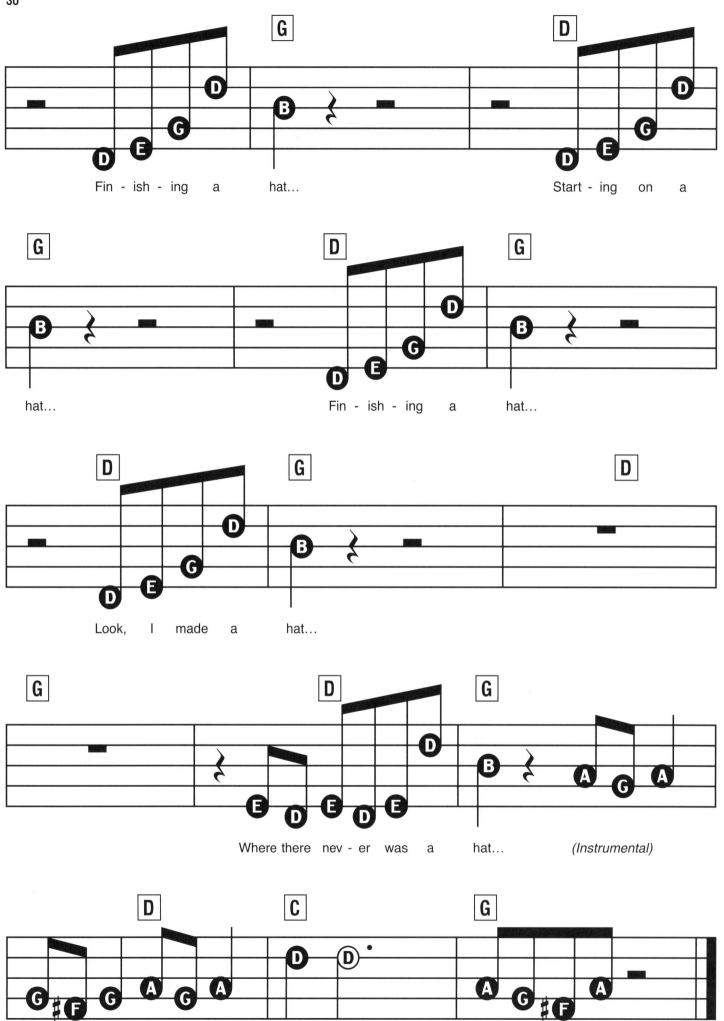

Me and the Sky
from COME FROM AWAY

Registration 4
Rhythm: Folk

Music and Lyrics by Irene Sankoff
and David Hein

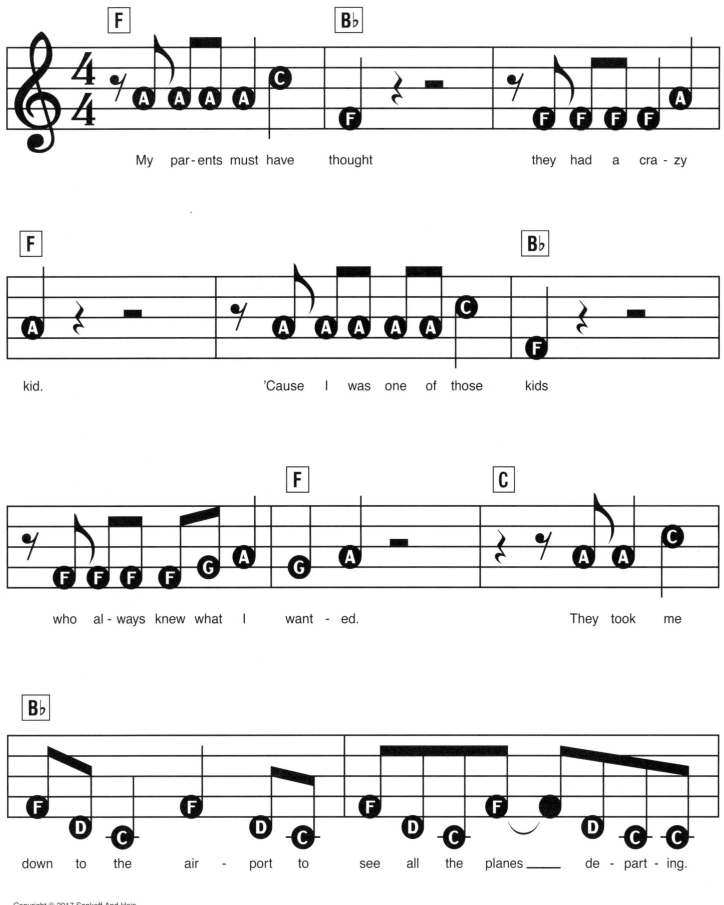

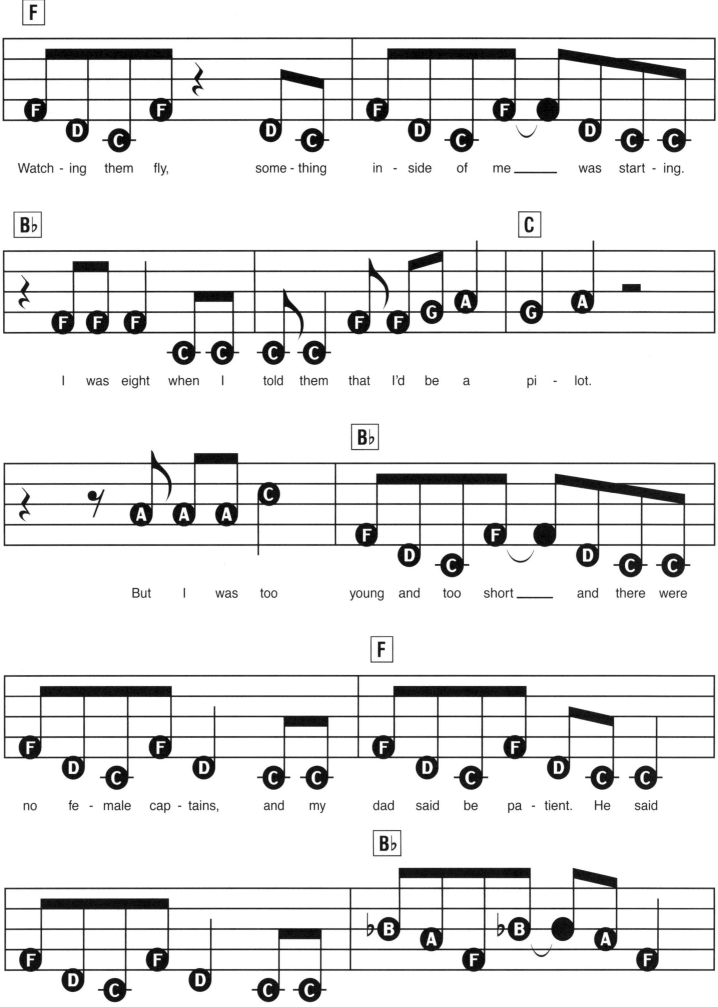

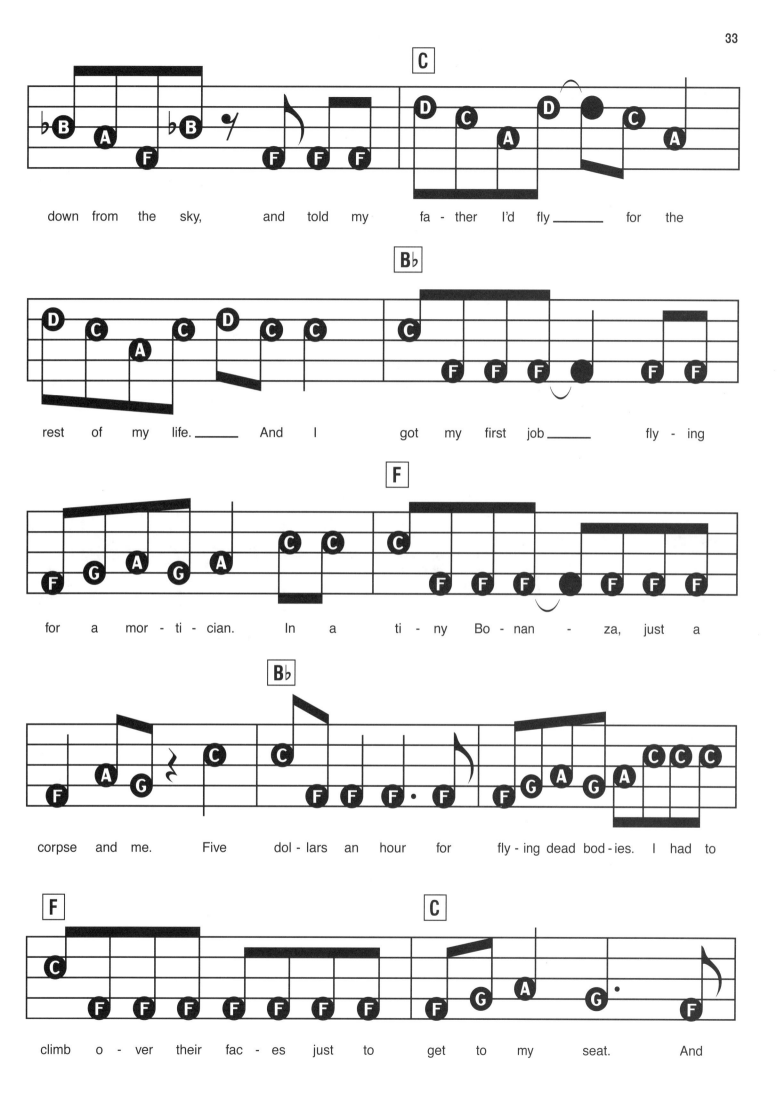

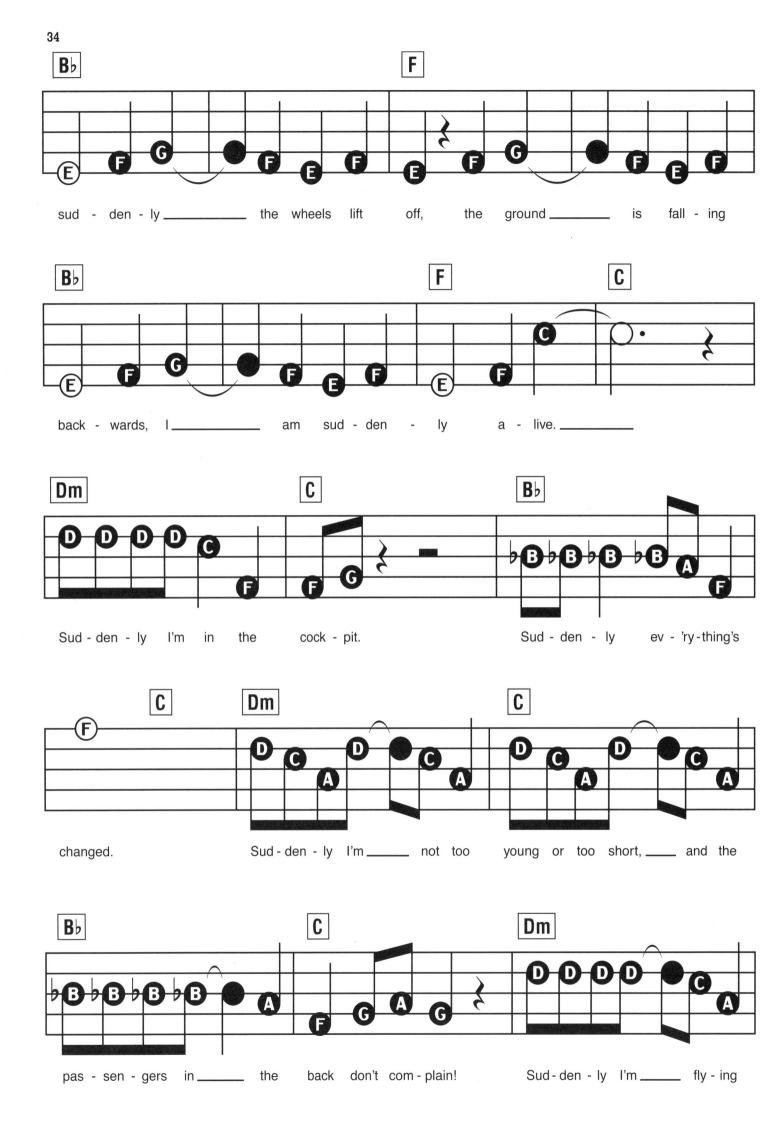

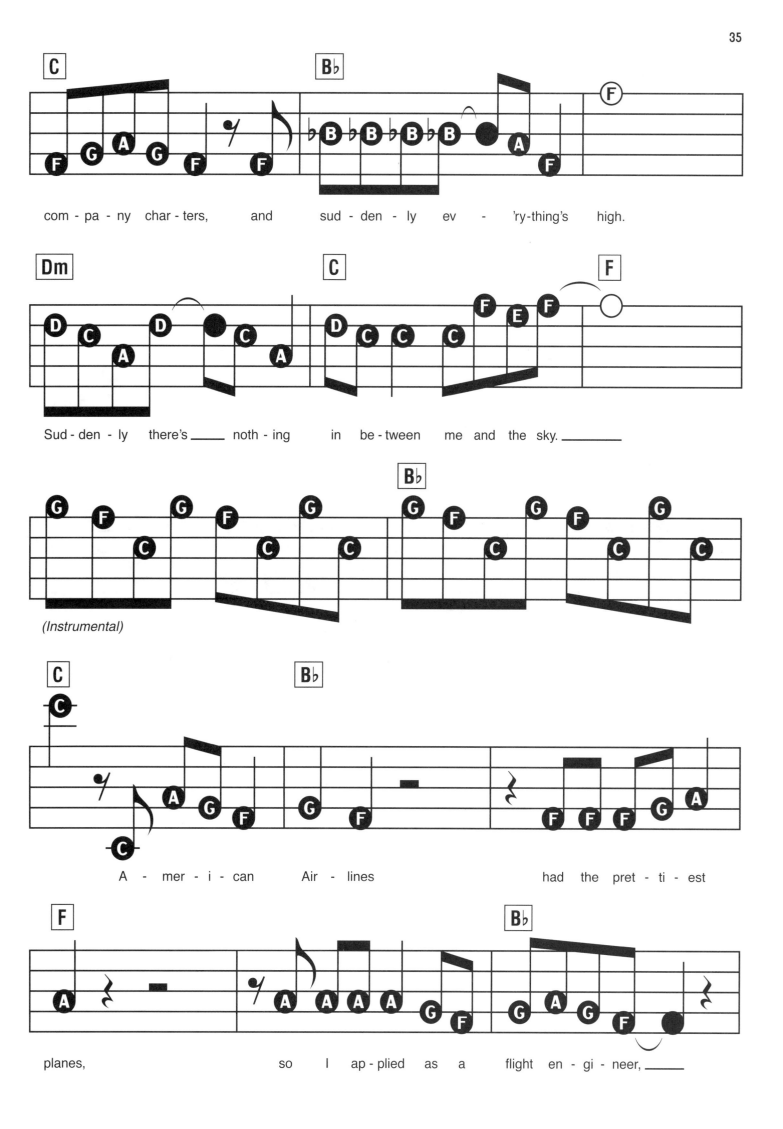

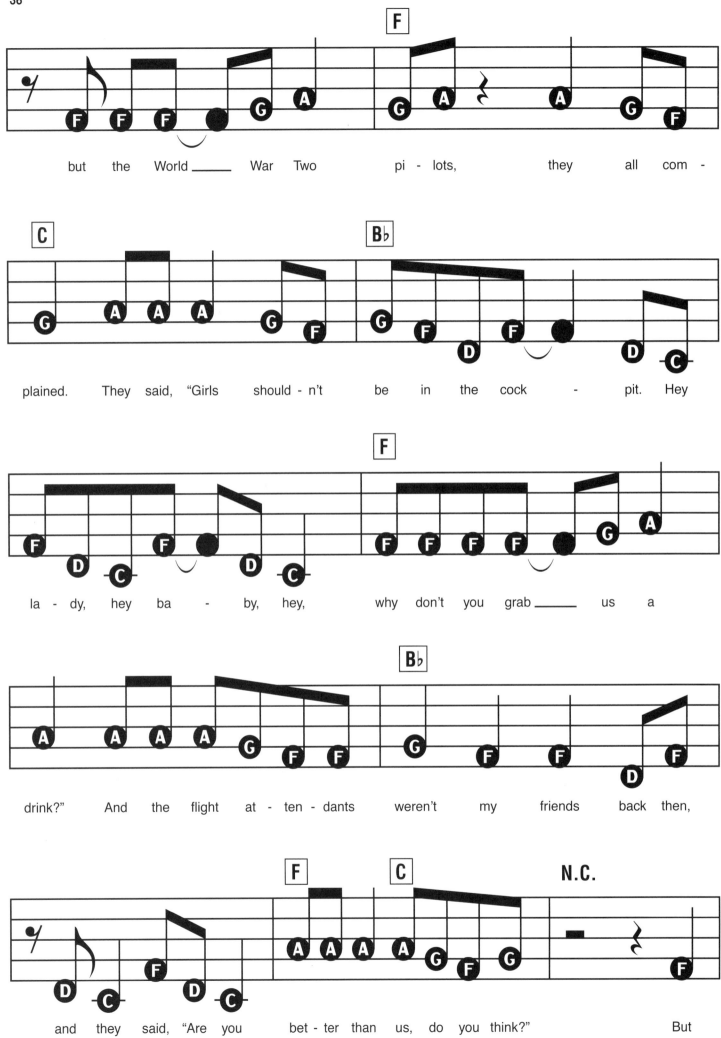

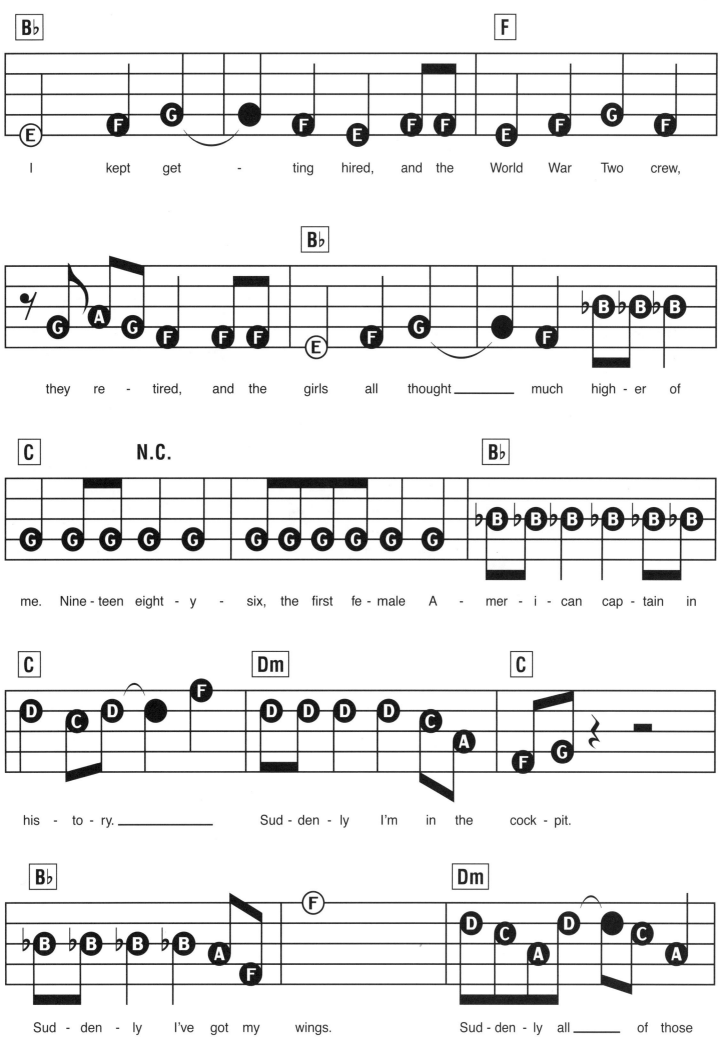

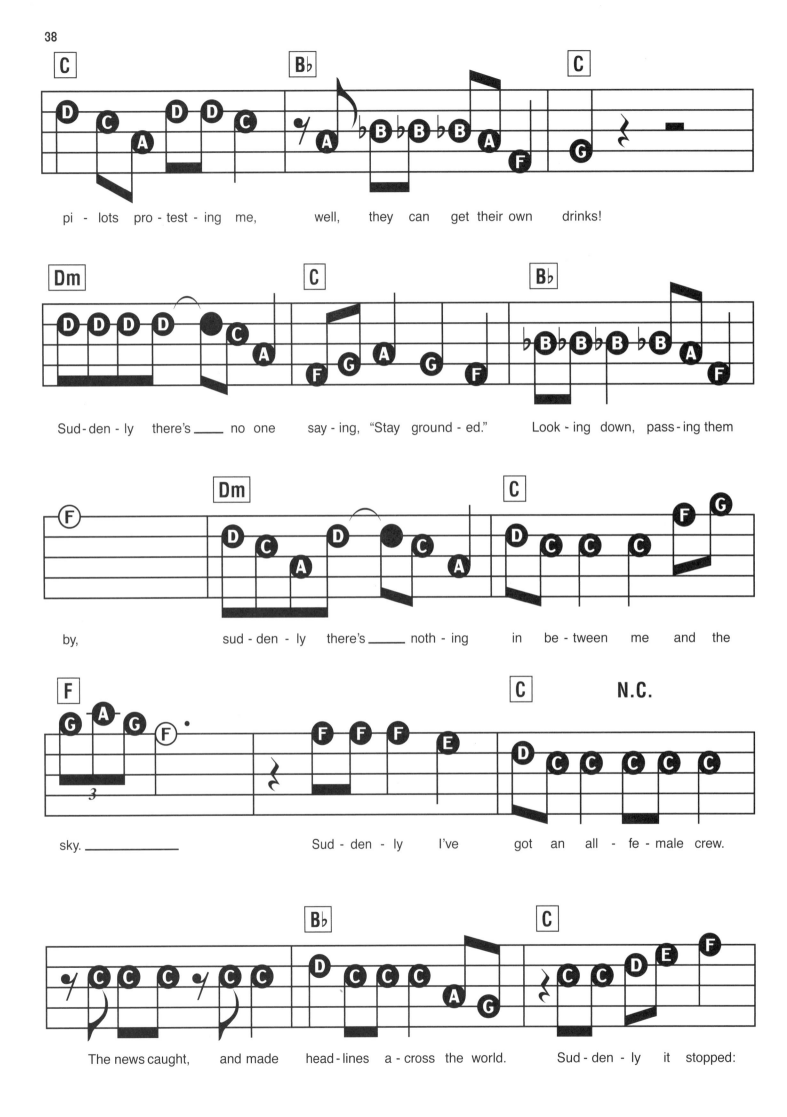

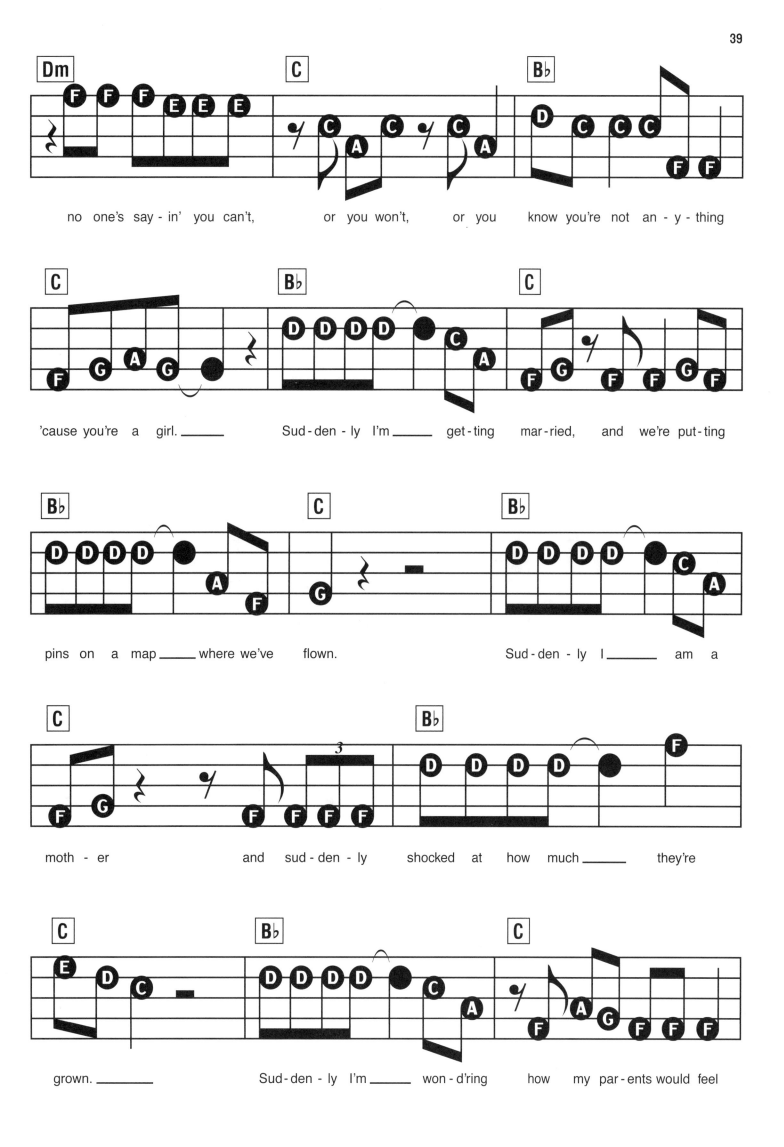

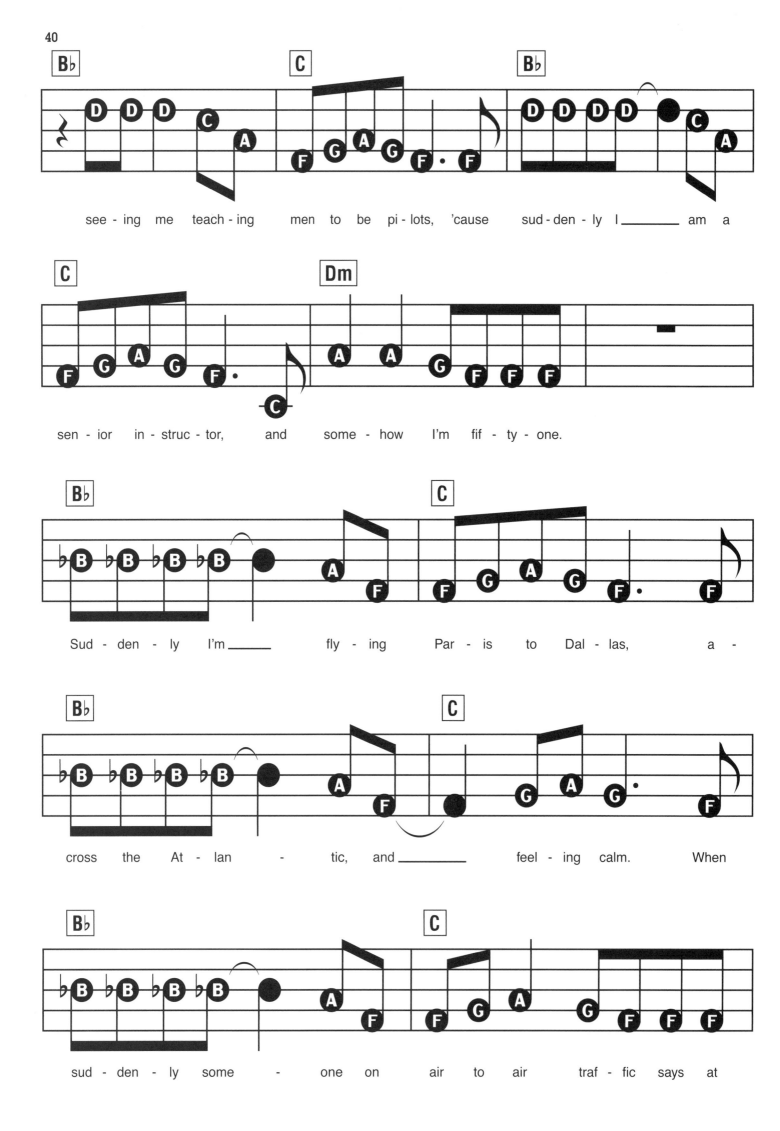

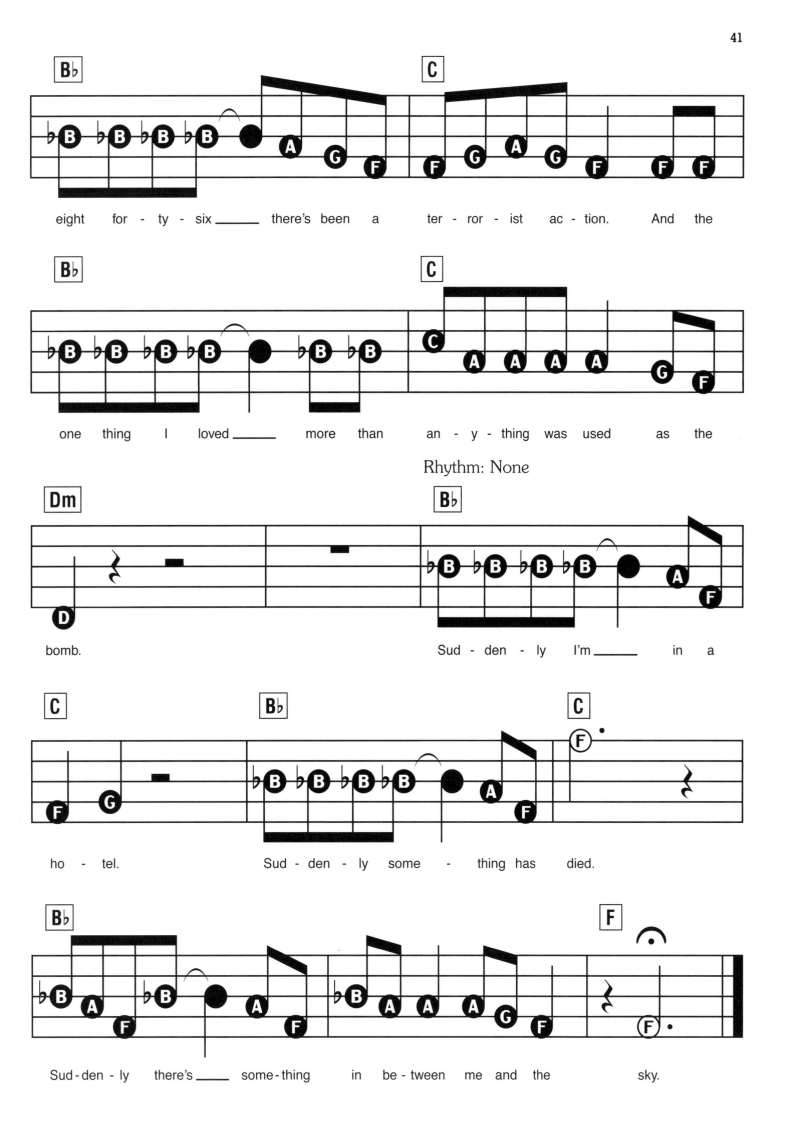

41

For Forever
from DEAR EVAN HANSEN

Registration 4
Rhythm: Bluegrass or Country

Music and Lyrics by Benj Pasek
and Justin Paul

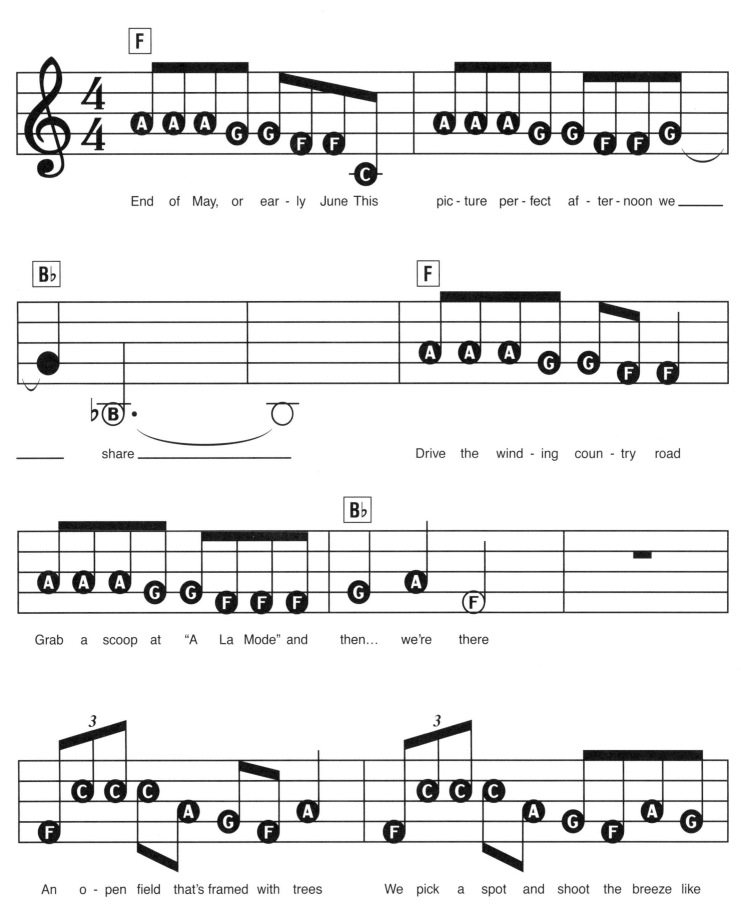

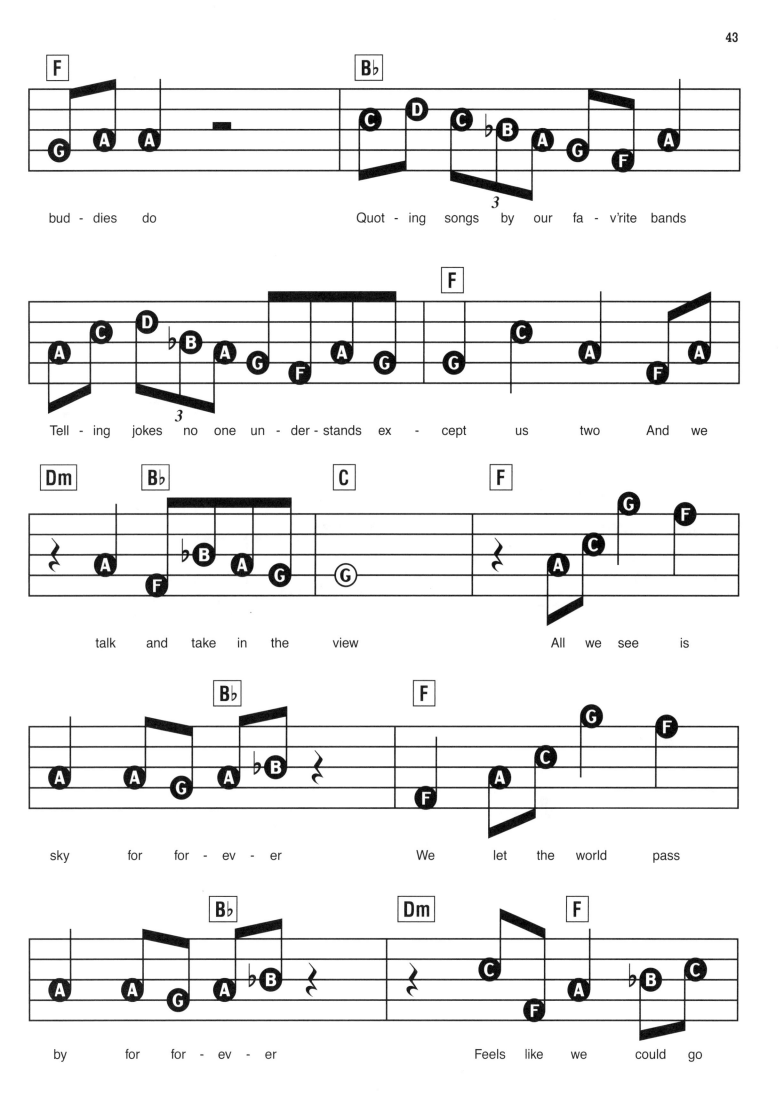

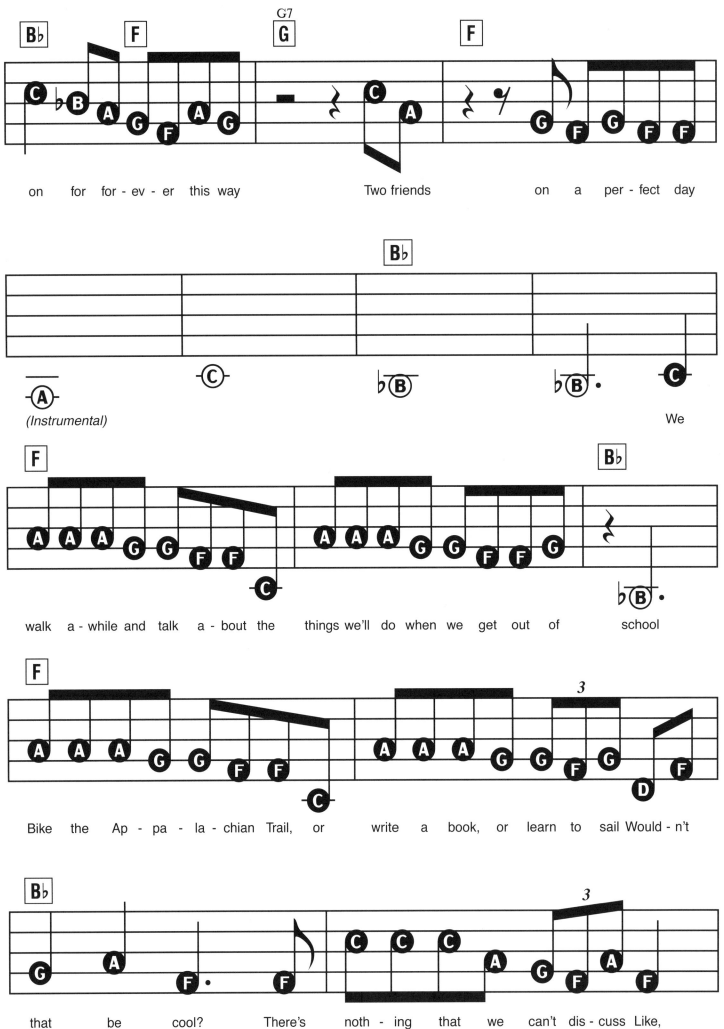

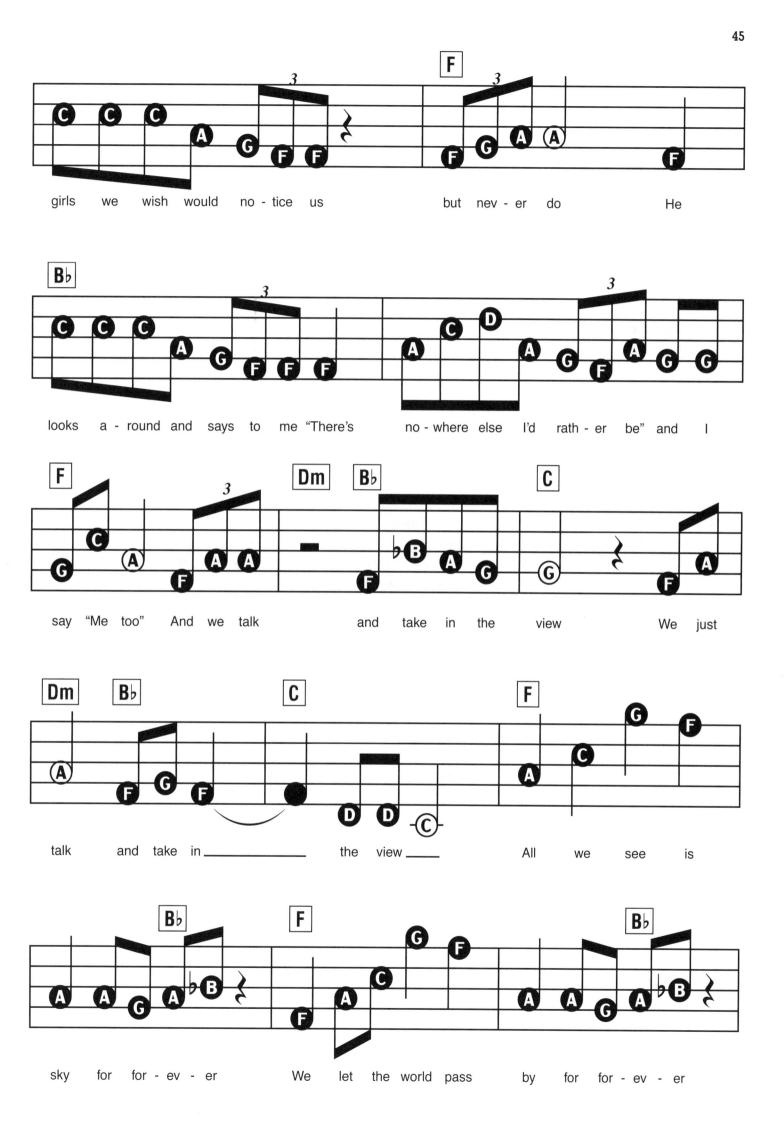

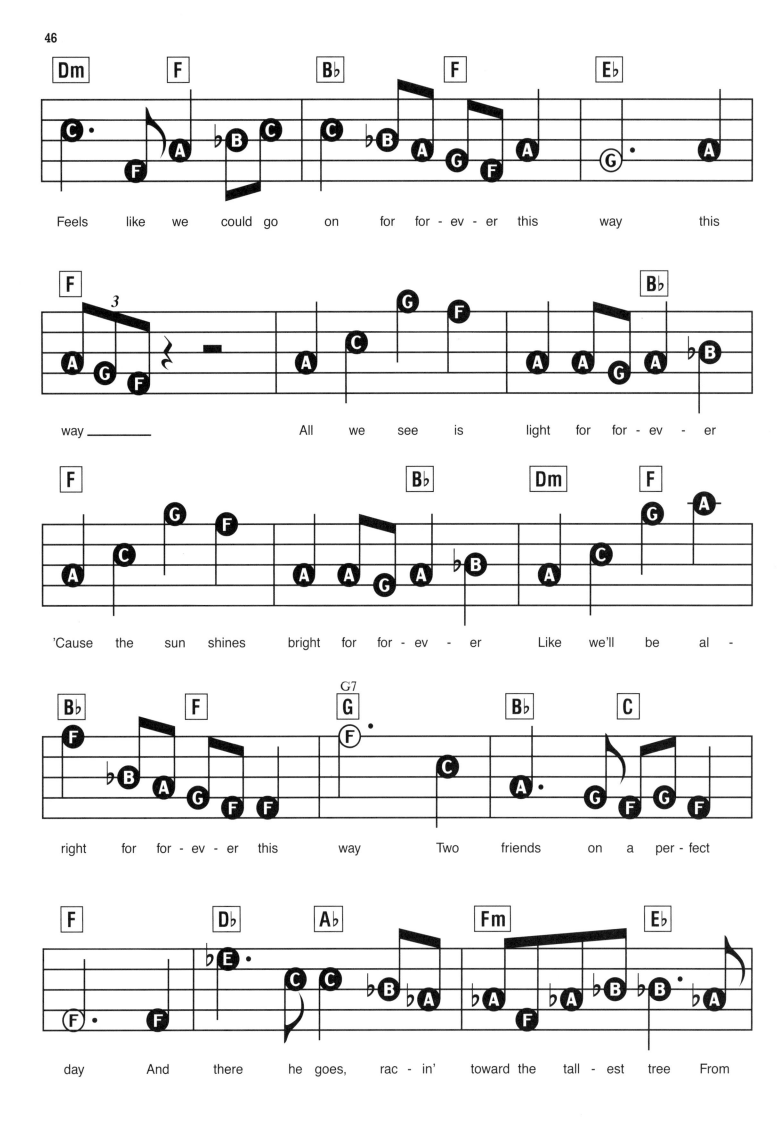

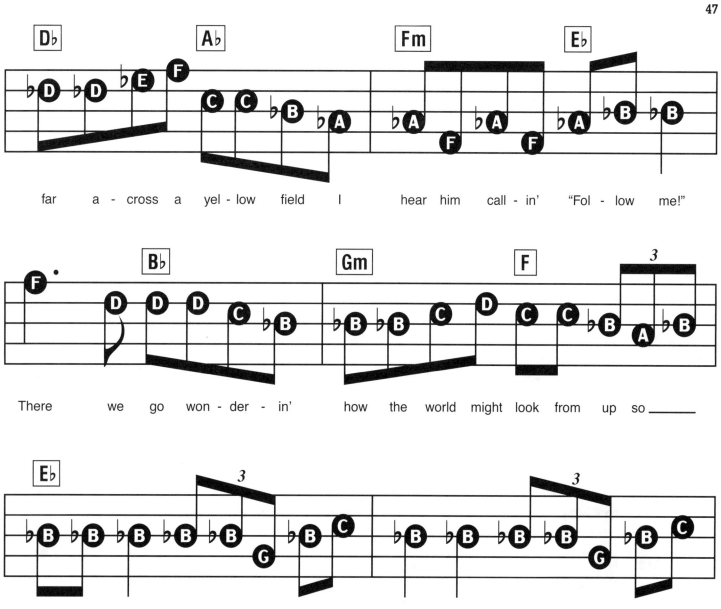

far a - cross a yel - low field I hear him call - in' "Fol - low me!"

There we go won - der - in' how the world might look from up so _____

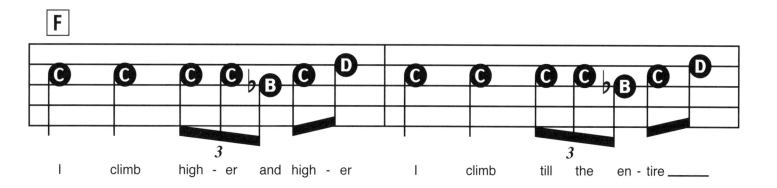

high One foot af - ter the oth - er One branch then to an - oth - er

I climb high - er and high - er I climb till the en - tire _____

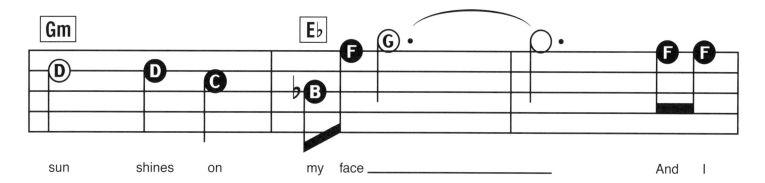

sun shines on my face _____ And I

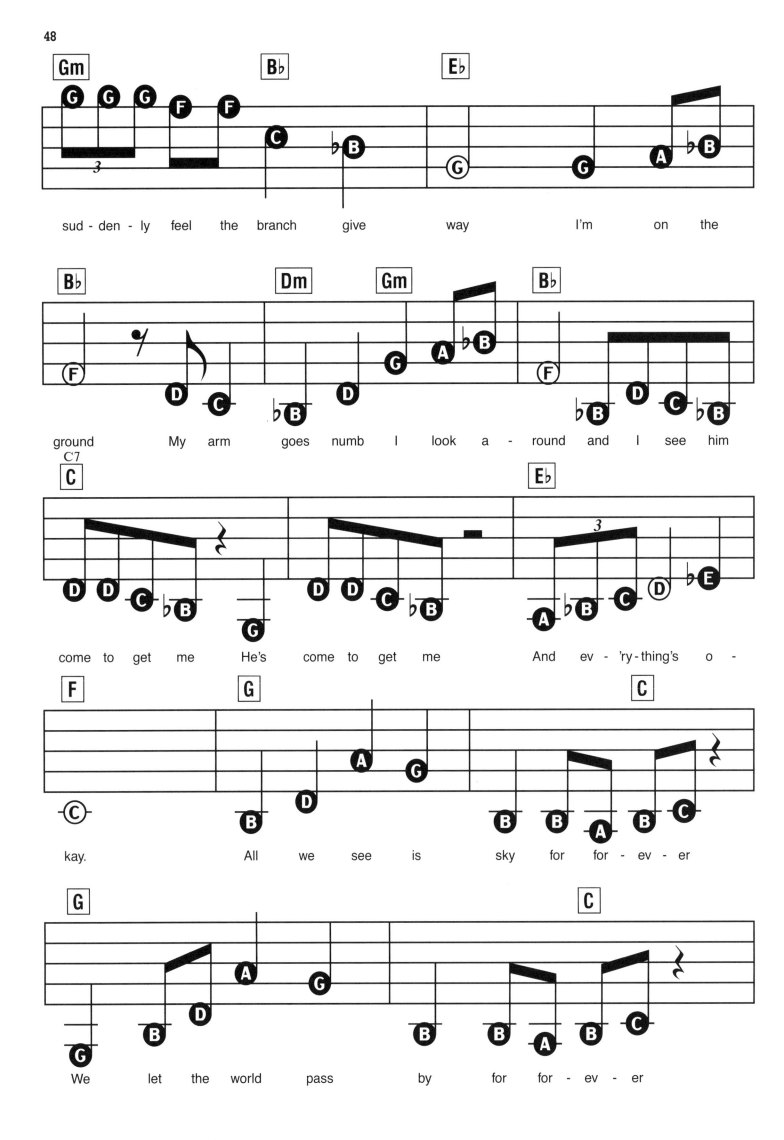

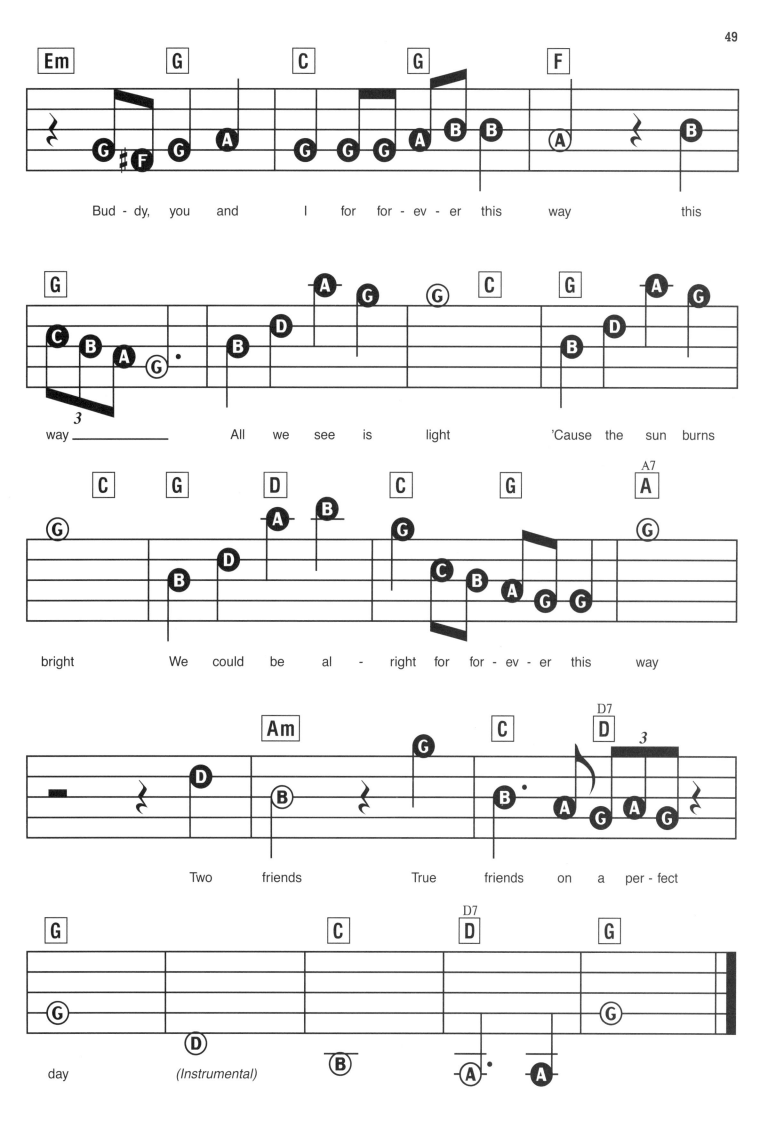

Getting to Know You
from THE KING AND I

Registration 8
Rhythm: Fox Trot or Swing

Lyrics by Oscar Hammerstein II
Music by Richard Rodgers

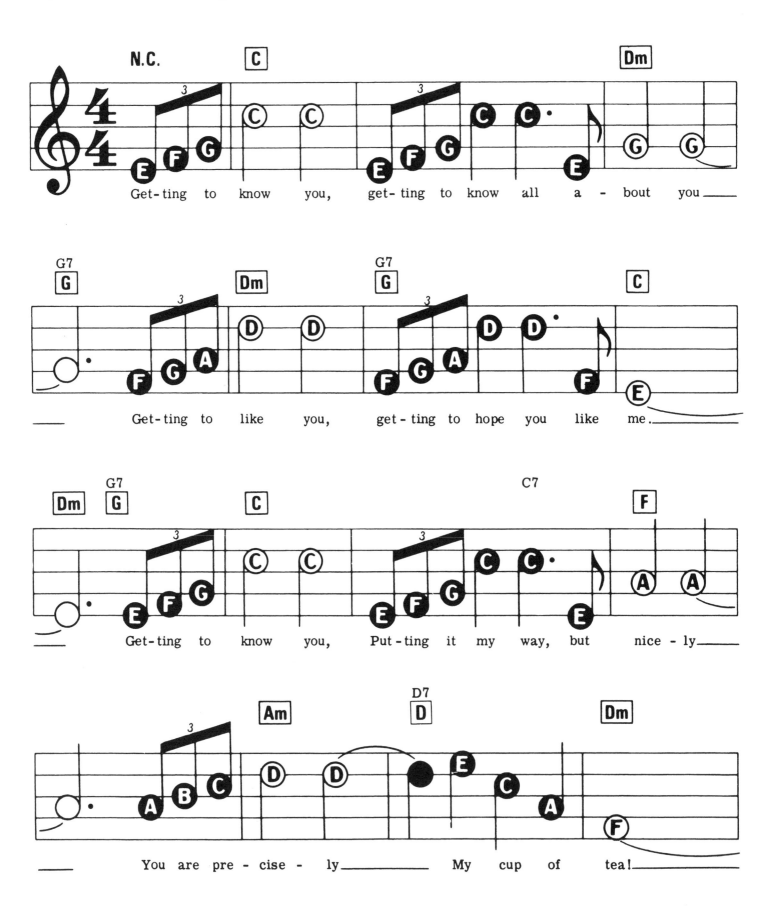

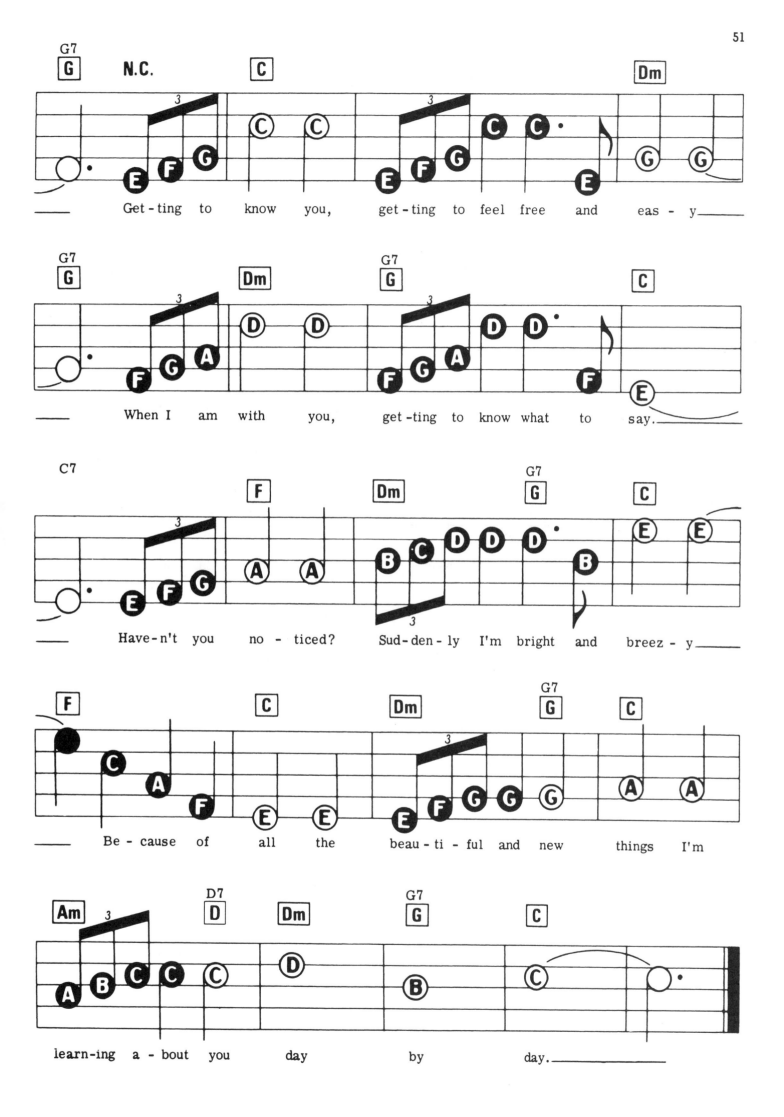

Hair
from the Broadway Musical Production HAIR

Registration 2
Rhythm: Broadway or Show Tunes

Words by James Rado and Gerome Ragni
Music by Galt MacDermot

She asks me why, I'm just a hair - y guy.

I'm hair - y noon and night, Hair that's a fright.

I'm hair - y high and low, Don't ask me why, don't know.

It's not for lack of bread. Like the Grate - ful Dead. Dar - lin',

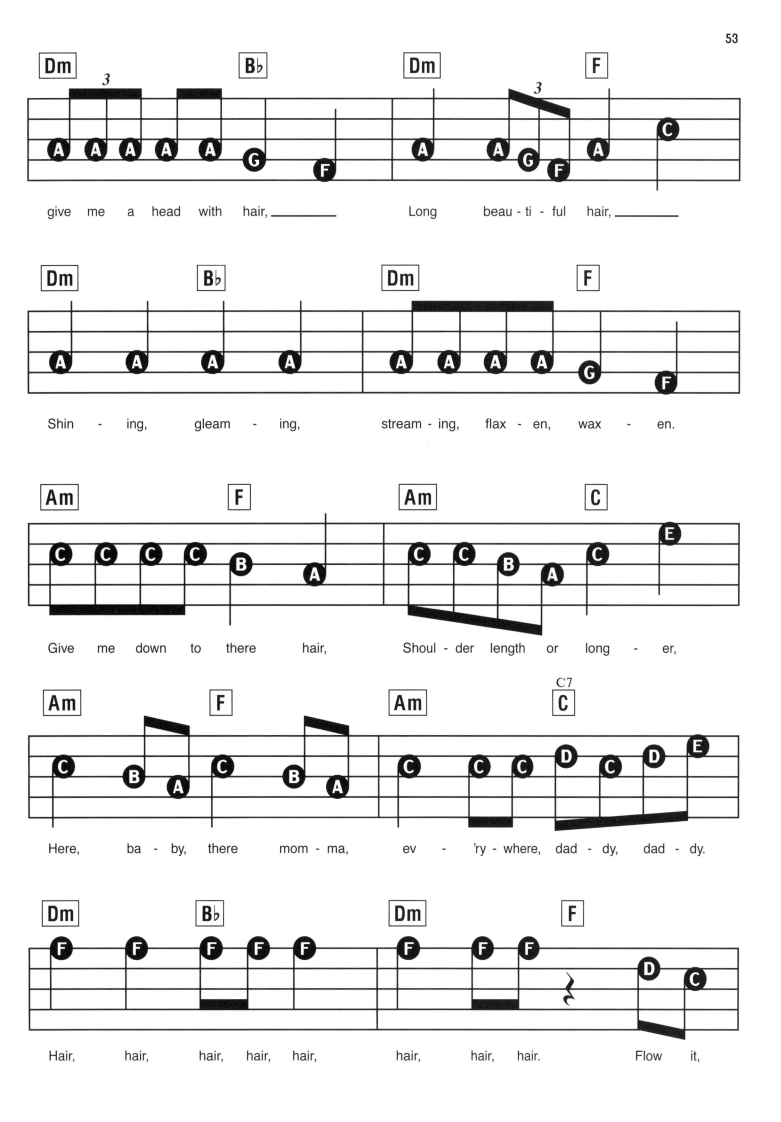

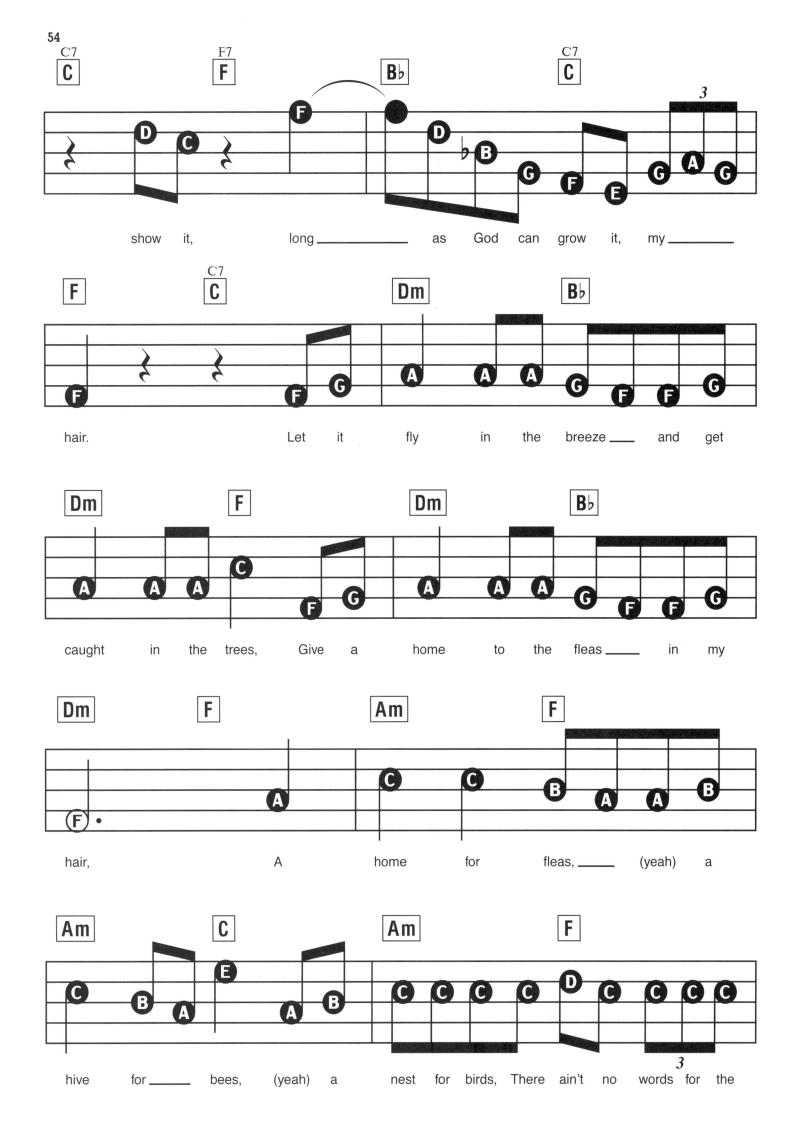

55

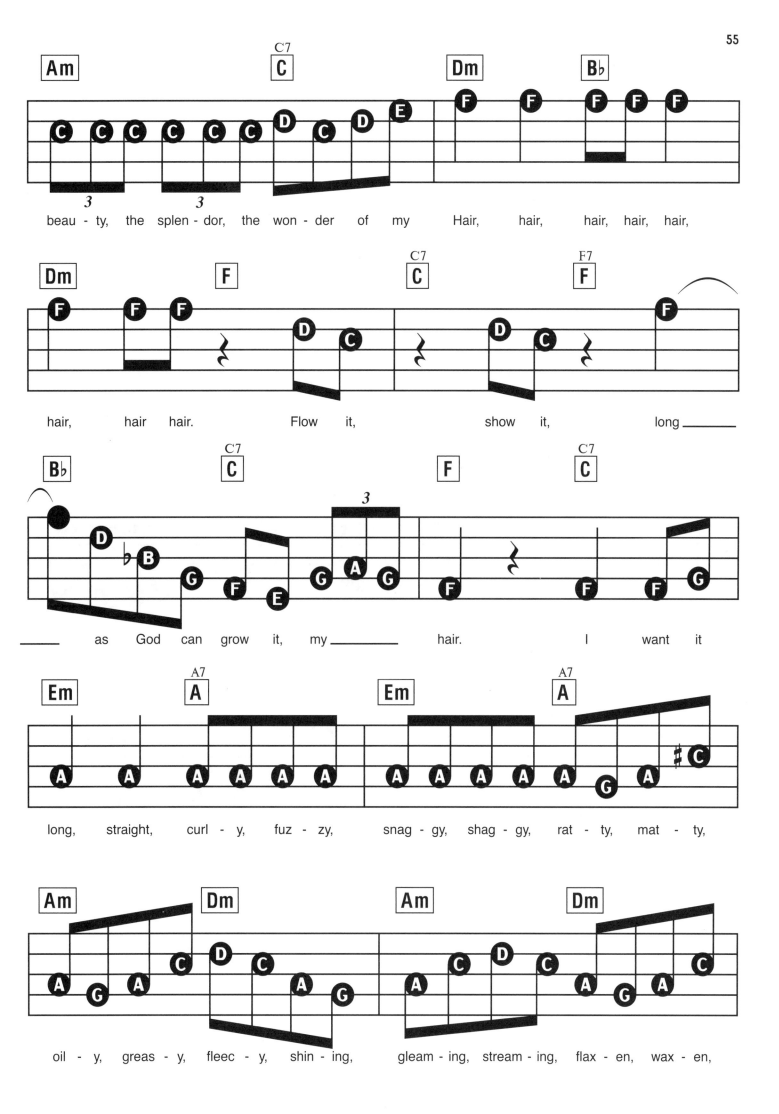

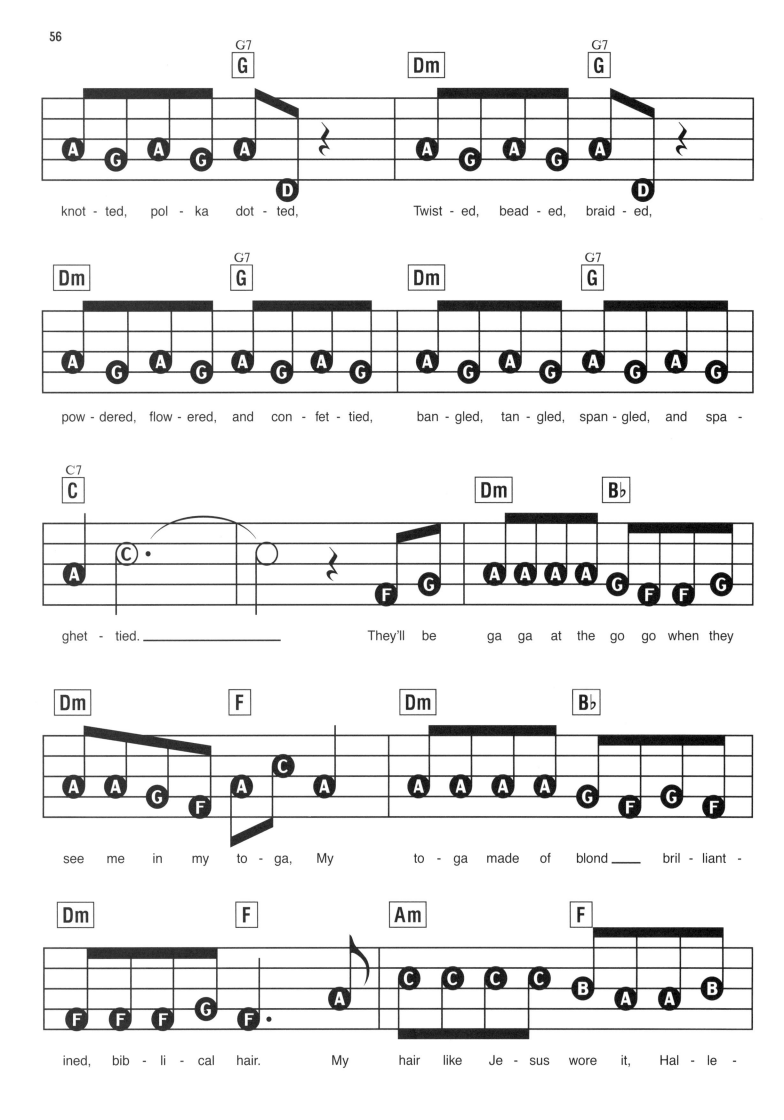

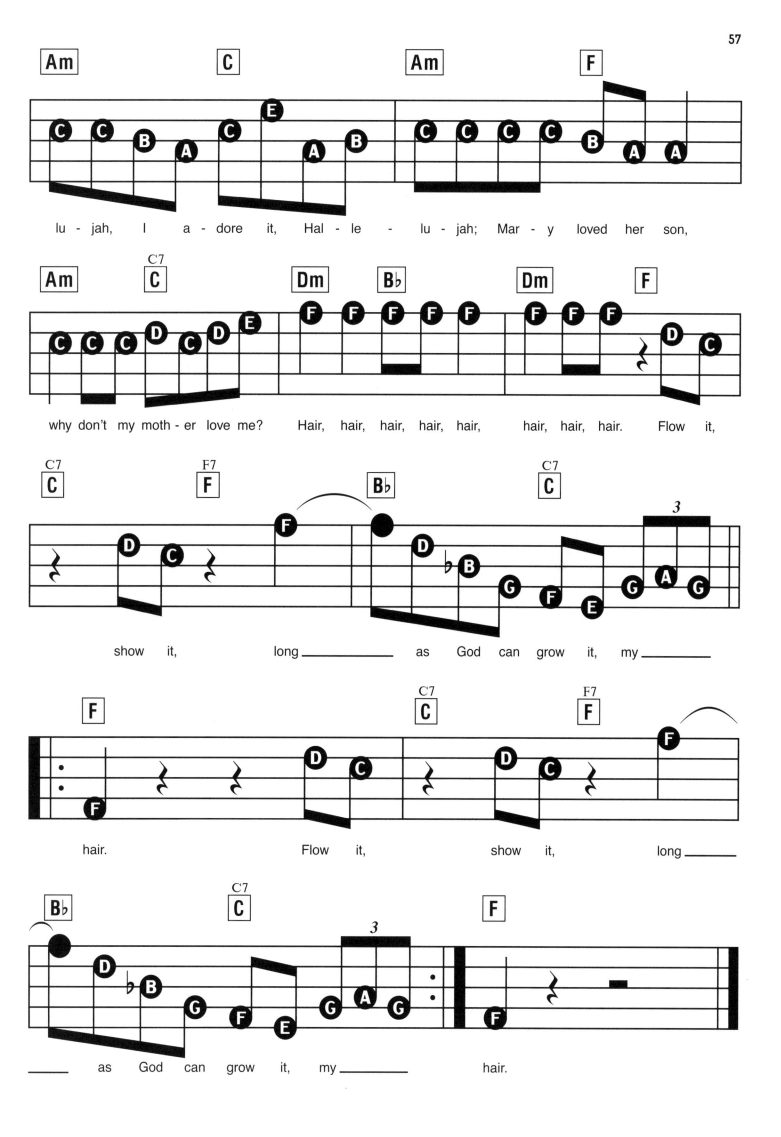

I Whistle a Happy Tune
from THE KING AND I

Registration 1
Rhythm: Fox Trot or Swing

Lyrics by Oscar Hammerstein II
Music by Richard Rodgers

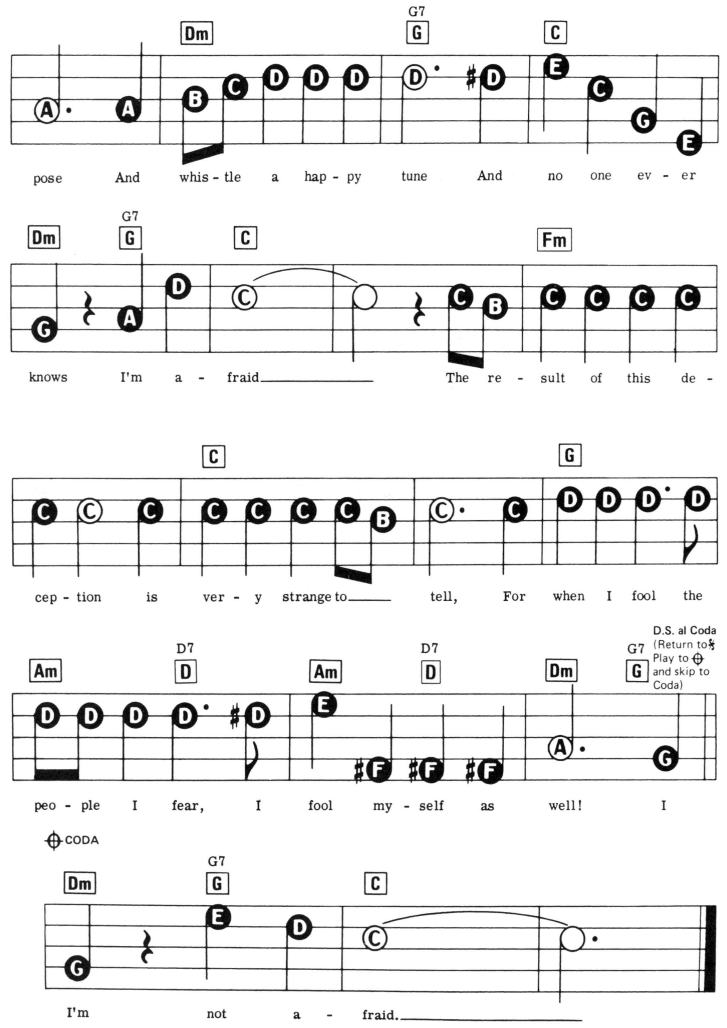

If I Were a Bell
from GUYS AND DOLLS

Registration 1
Rhythm: Fox Trot, Swing or Polka

By Frank Loesser

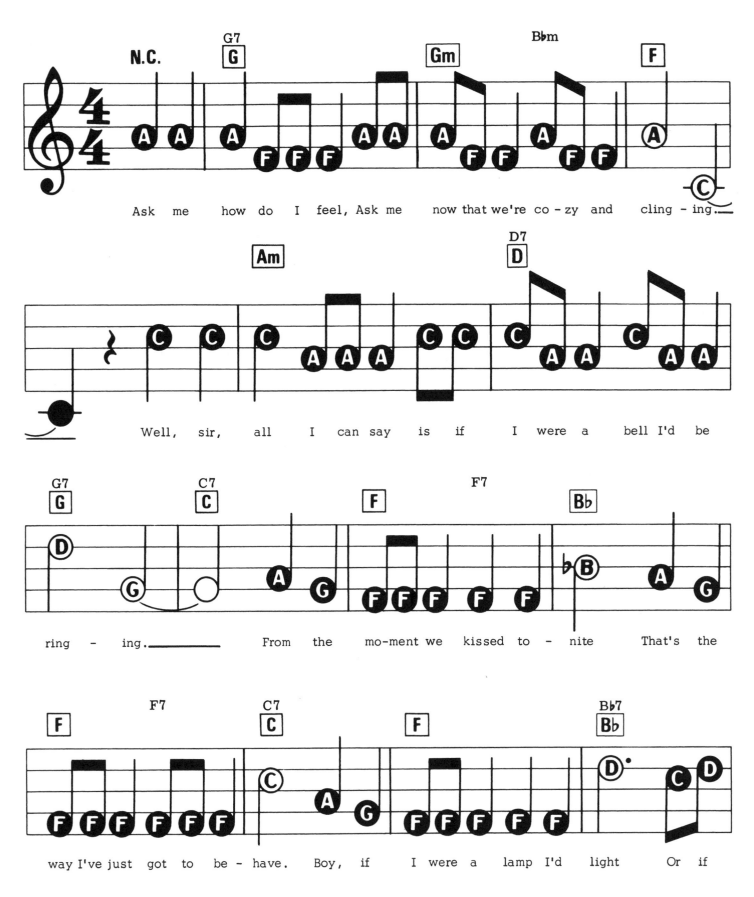

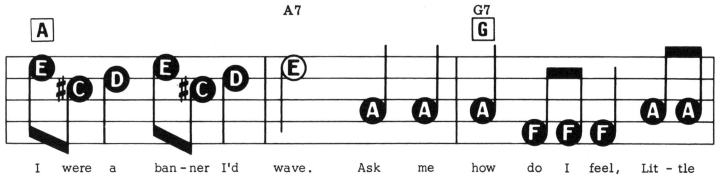

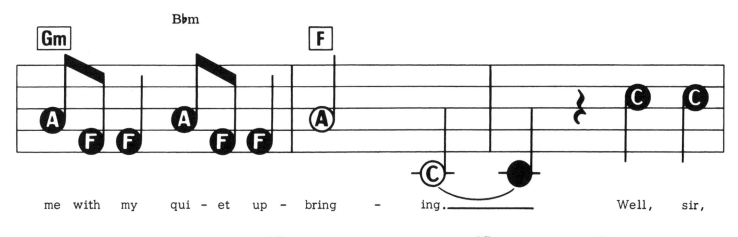

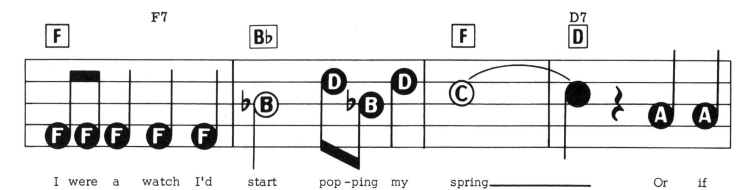

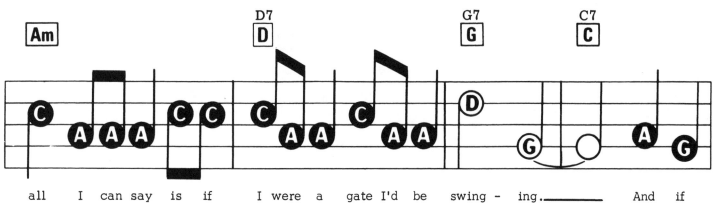

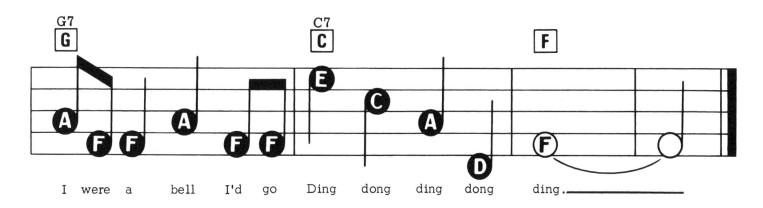

It Might as Well Be Spring
from STATE FAIR

Registration 3
Rhythm: Ballad

Lyrics by Oscar Hammerstein II
Music by Richard Rodgers

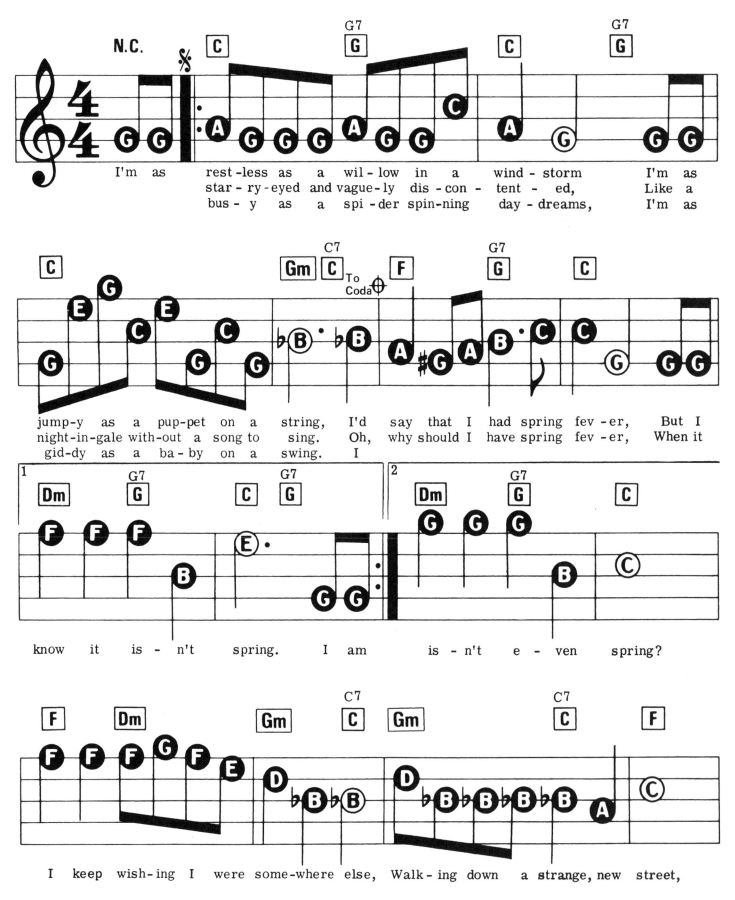

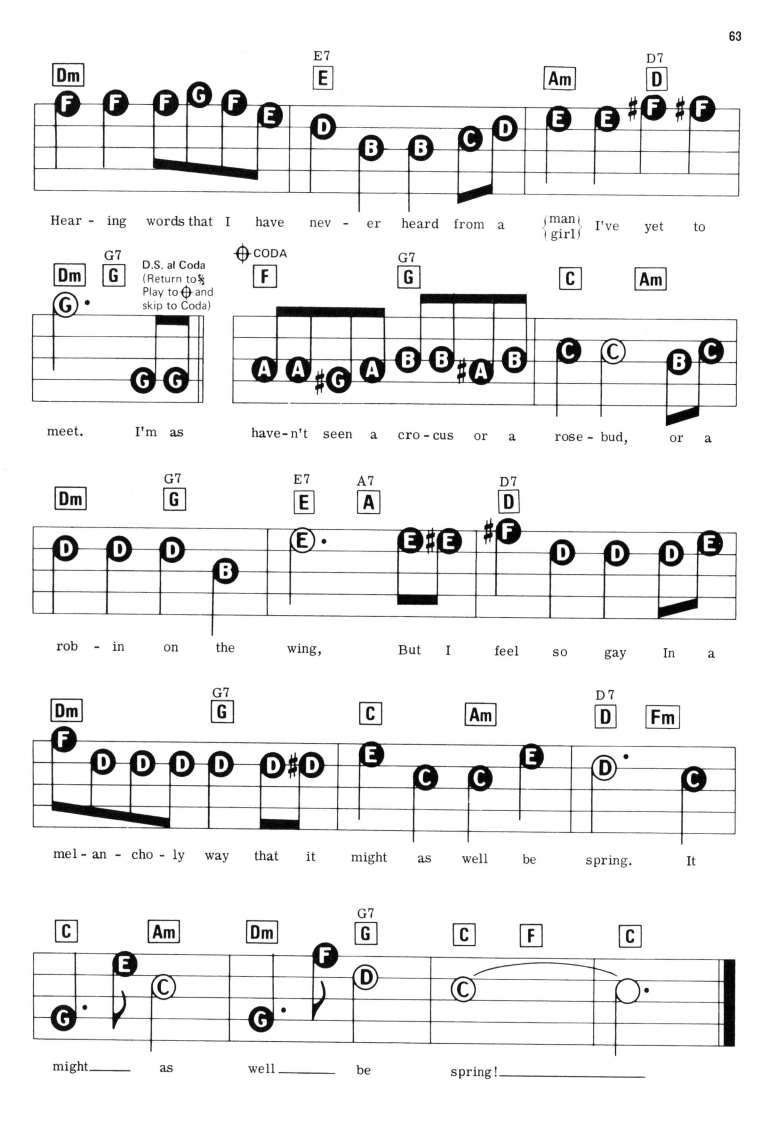

Hear - ing words that I have nev - er heard from a {man}{girl} I've yet to

meet. I'm as have-n't seen a cro-cus or a rose - bud, or a

rob - in on the wing, But I feel so gay In a

mel - an - cho - ly way that it might as well be spring. It

might_____ as well_____ be spring!_____

My Favorite Things
from THE SOUND OF MUSIC

Registration 1
Rhythm: Waltz

Lyrics by Oscar Hammerstein II
Music by Richard Rodgers

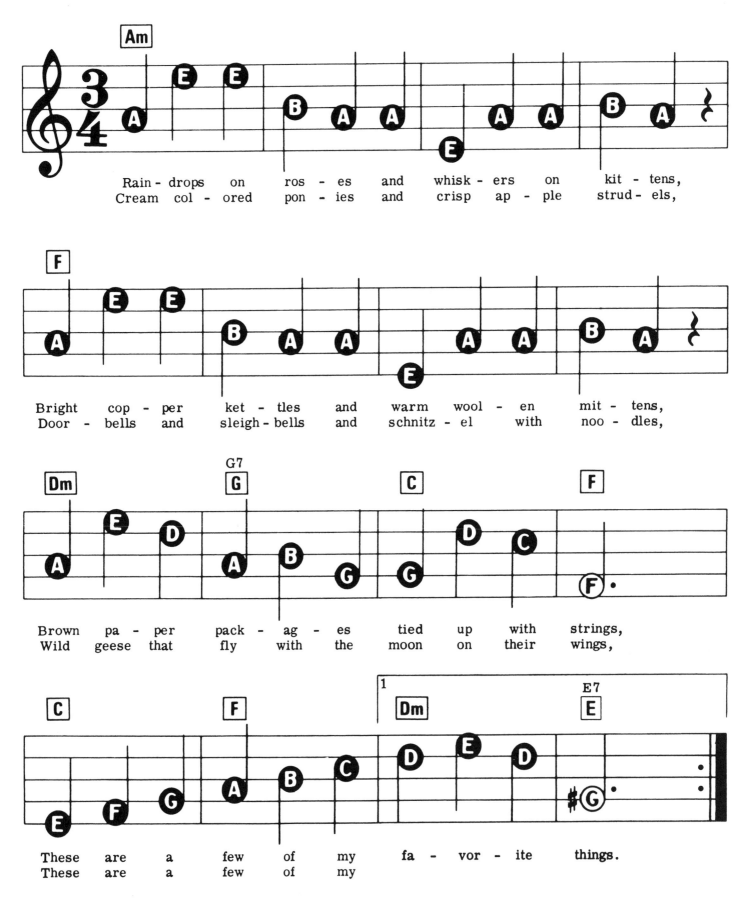

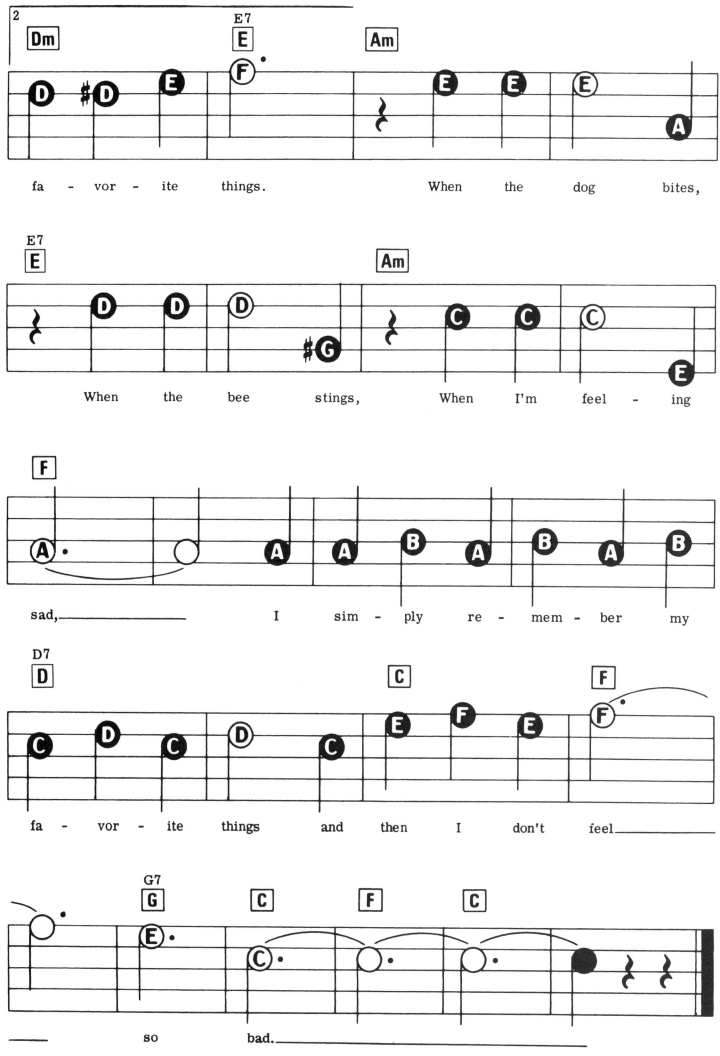

Oh, What a Beautiful Mornin'
from OKLAHOMA!

Registration 5
Rhythm: Waltz

Lyrics by Oscar Hammerstein II
Music by Richard Rodgers

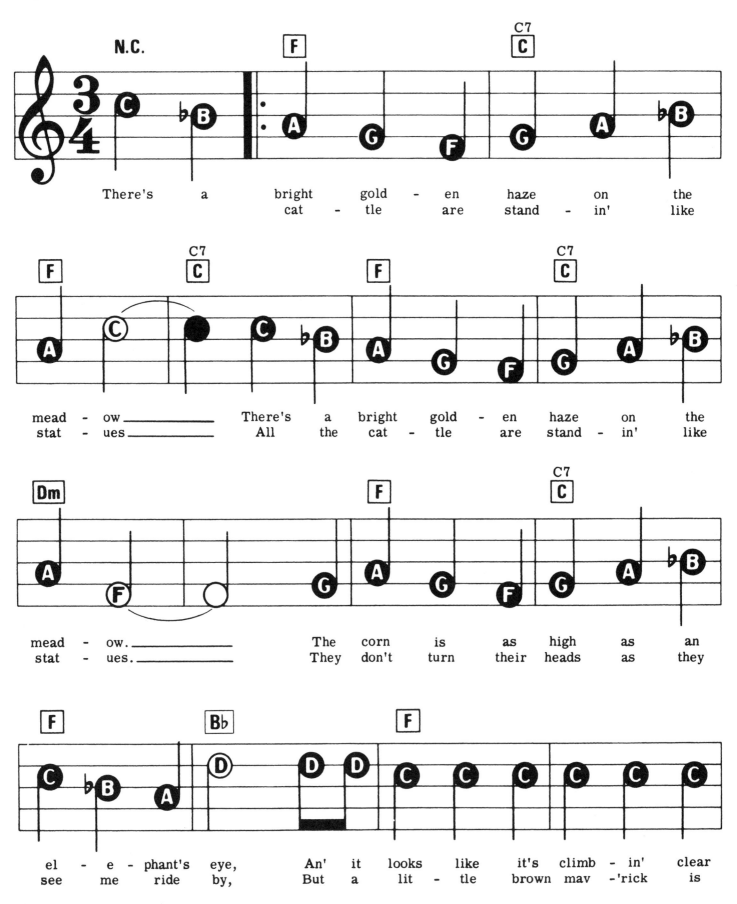

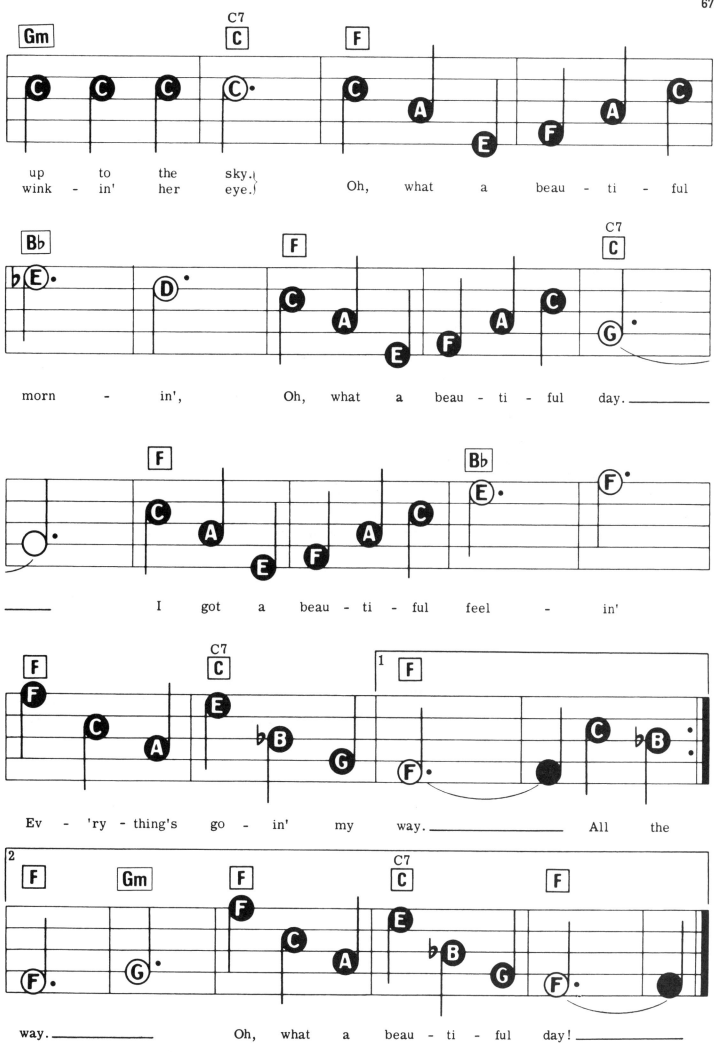

Pink
from WAR PAINT

Registration 2
Rhythm: None

Music by Scott Frankel
Lyrics by Michael Korie

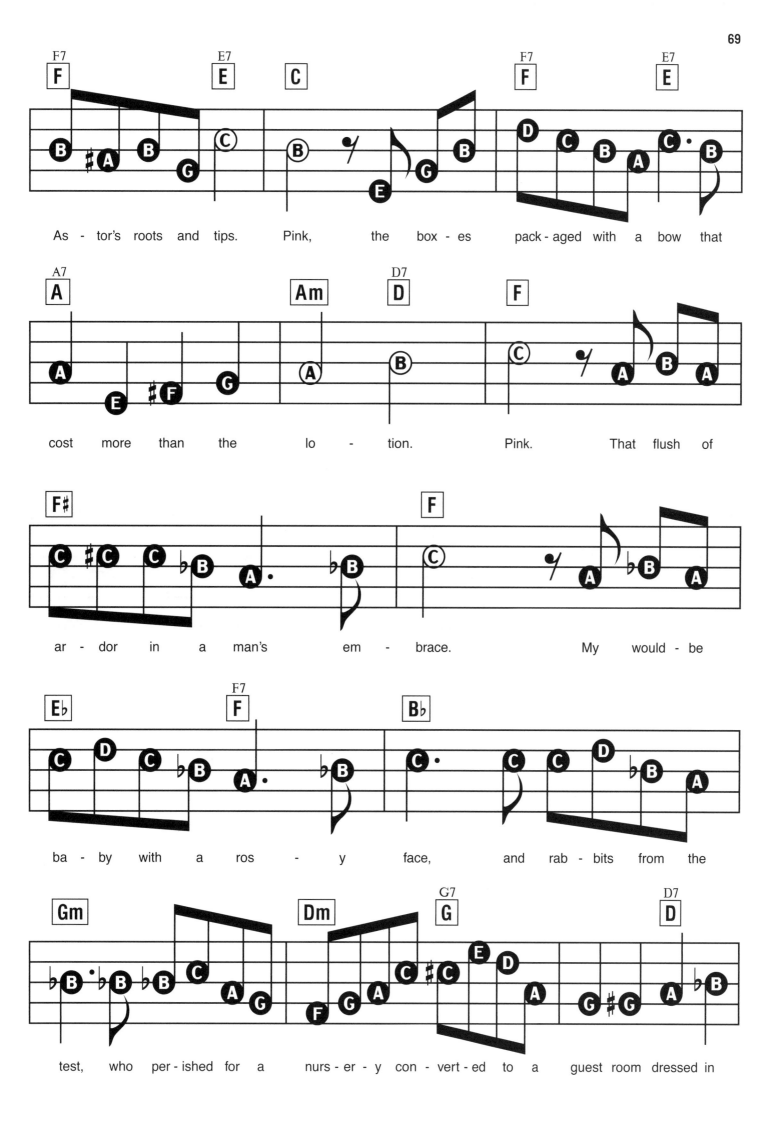

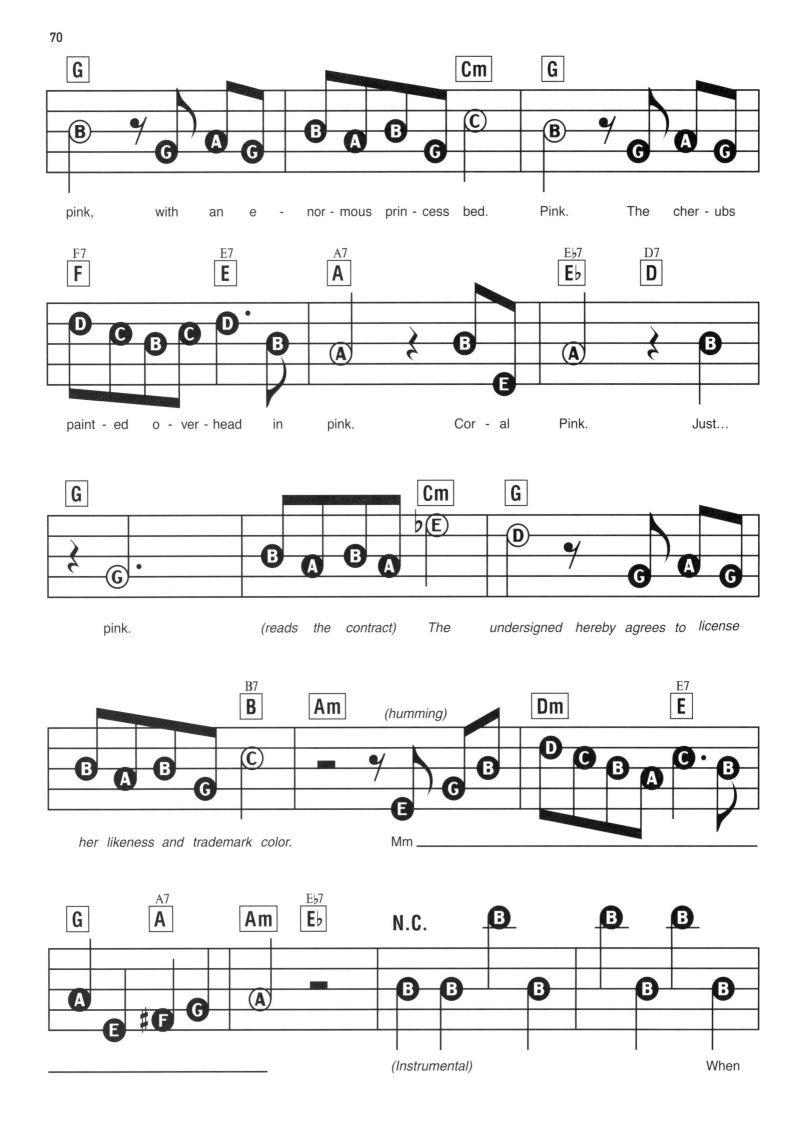

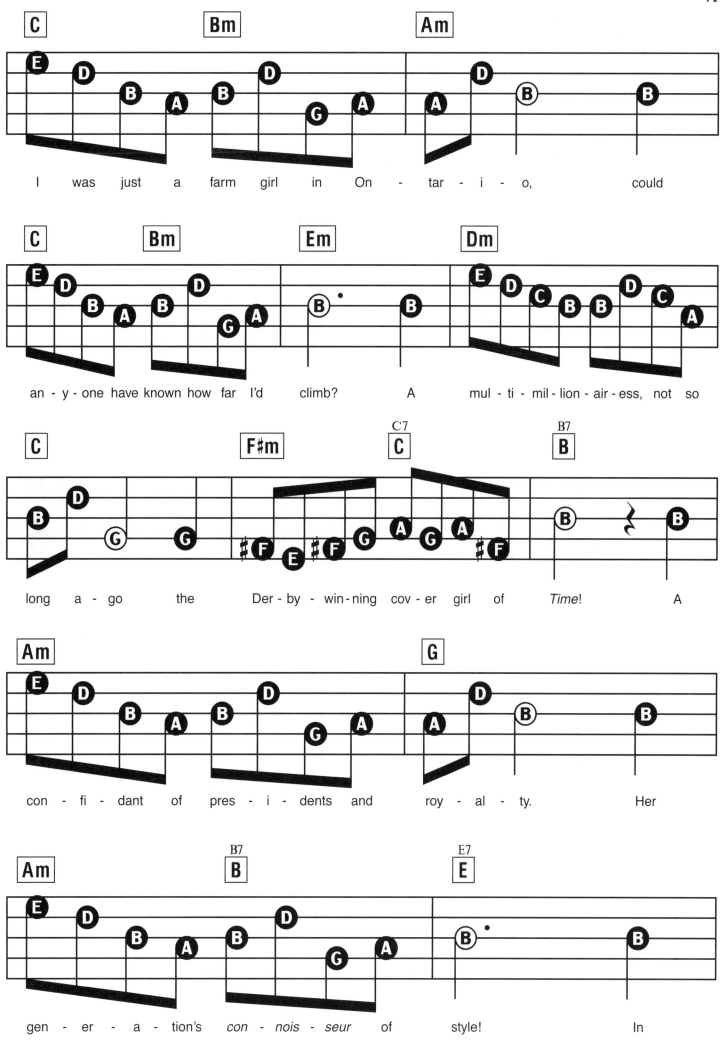

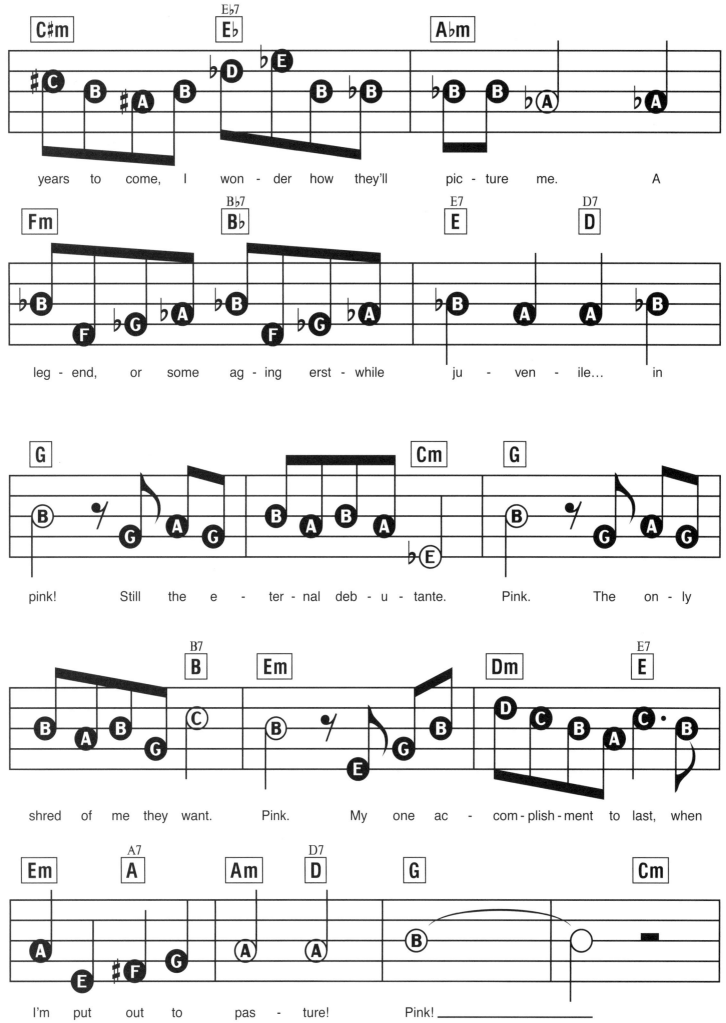

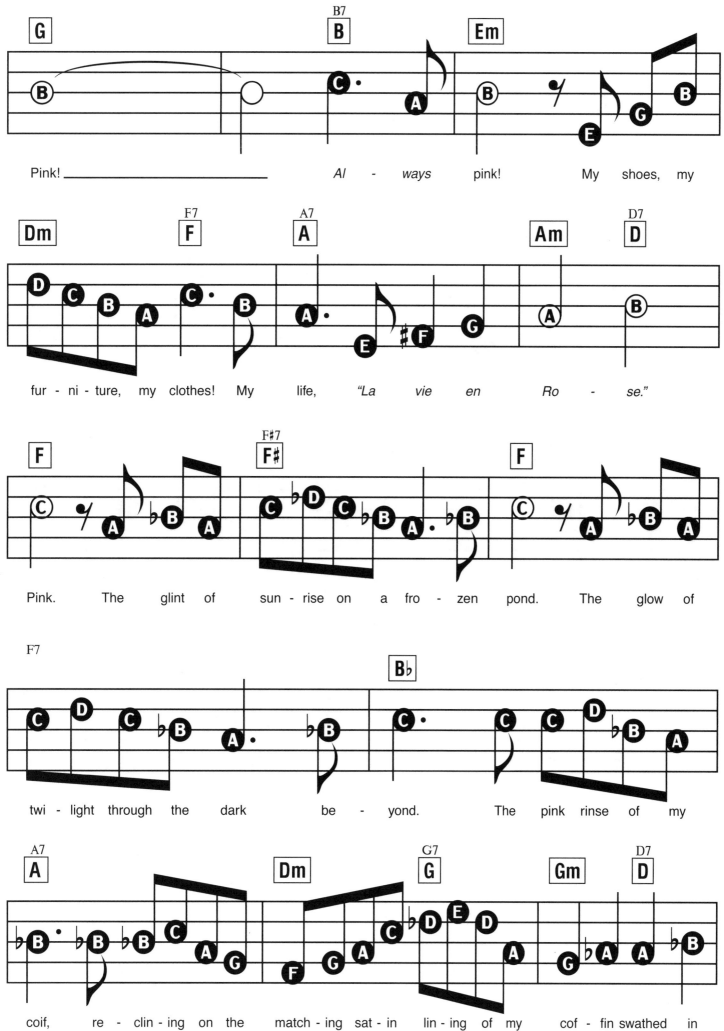

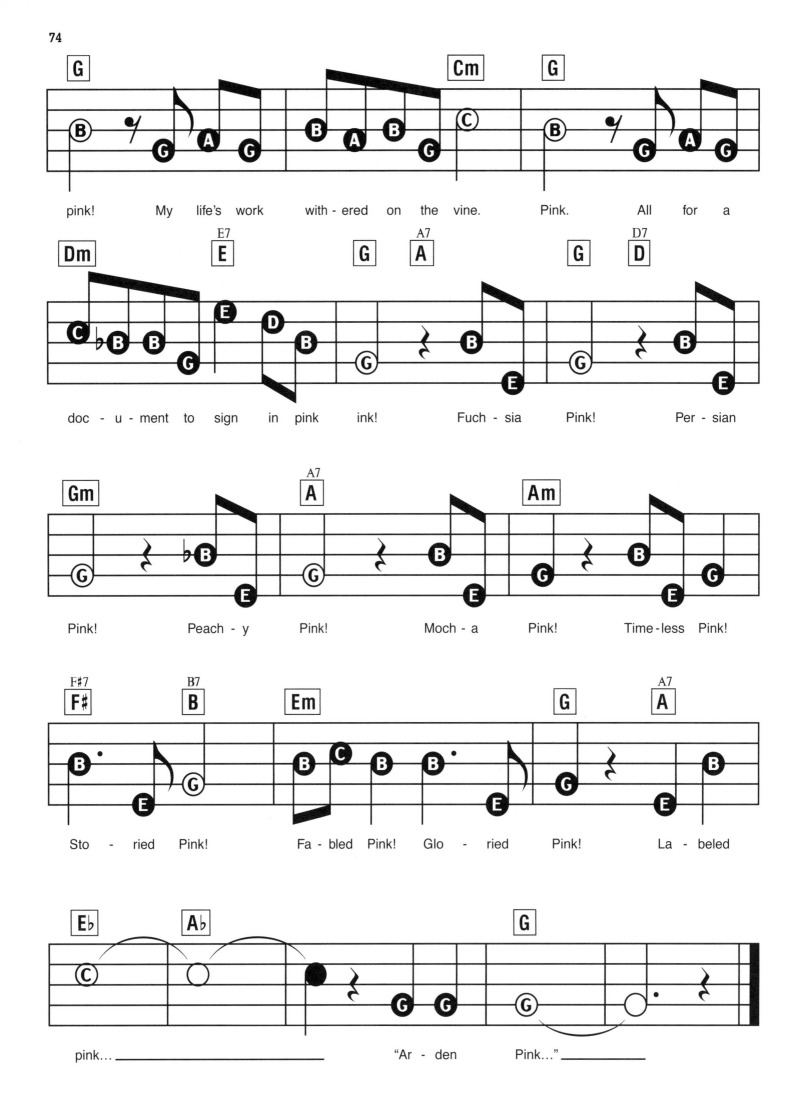

Put On Your Sunday Clothes
from HELLO, DOLLY!

Registration 2
Rhythm: Broadway or Fox Trot

Music and Lyric by
Jerry Herman

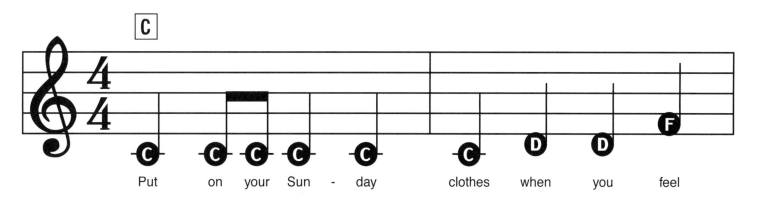

Put on your Sun - day clothes when you feel

down and out, _____ strut down the street and

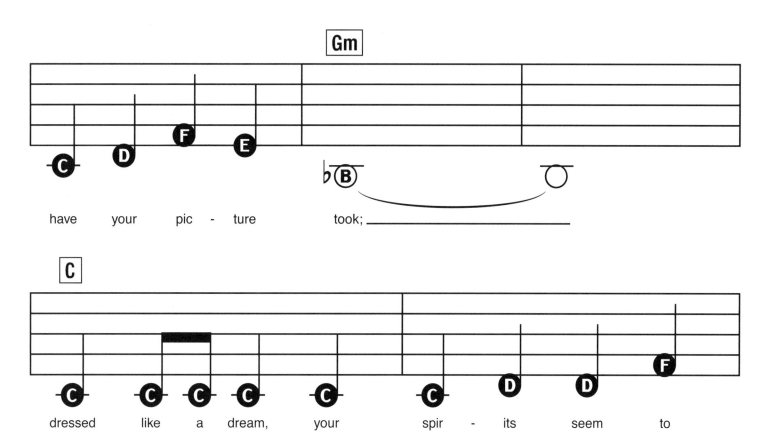

have your pic - ture took; _____

dressed like a dream, your spir - its seem to

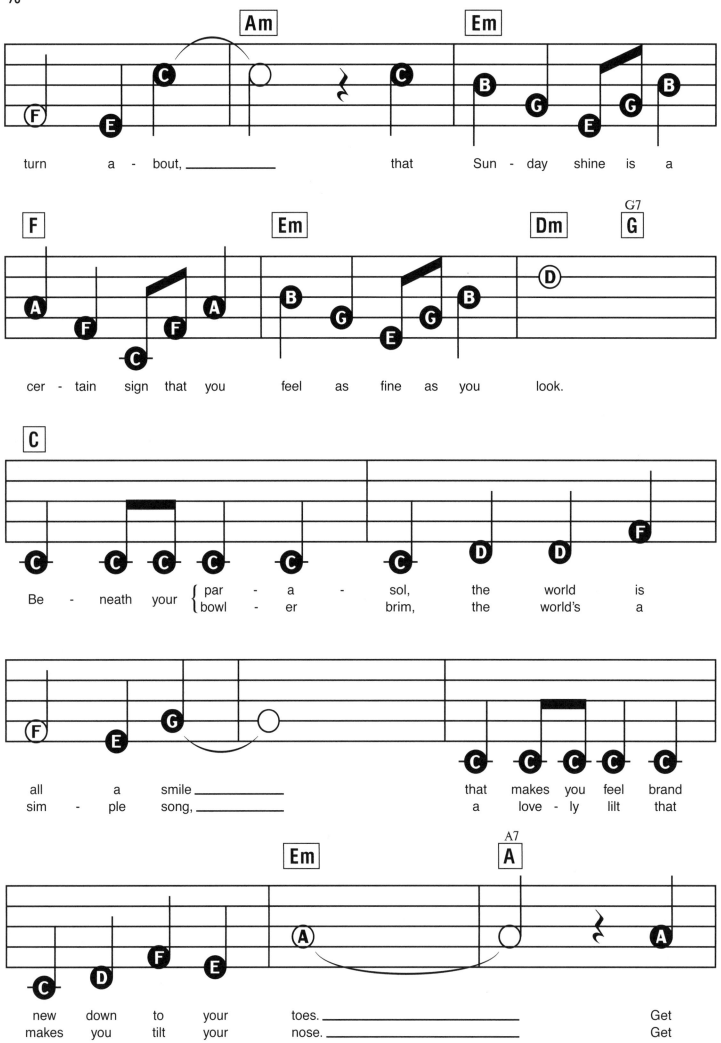

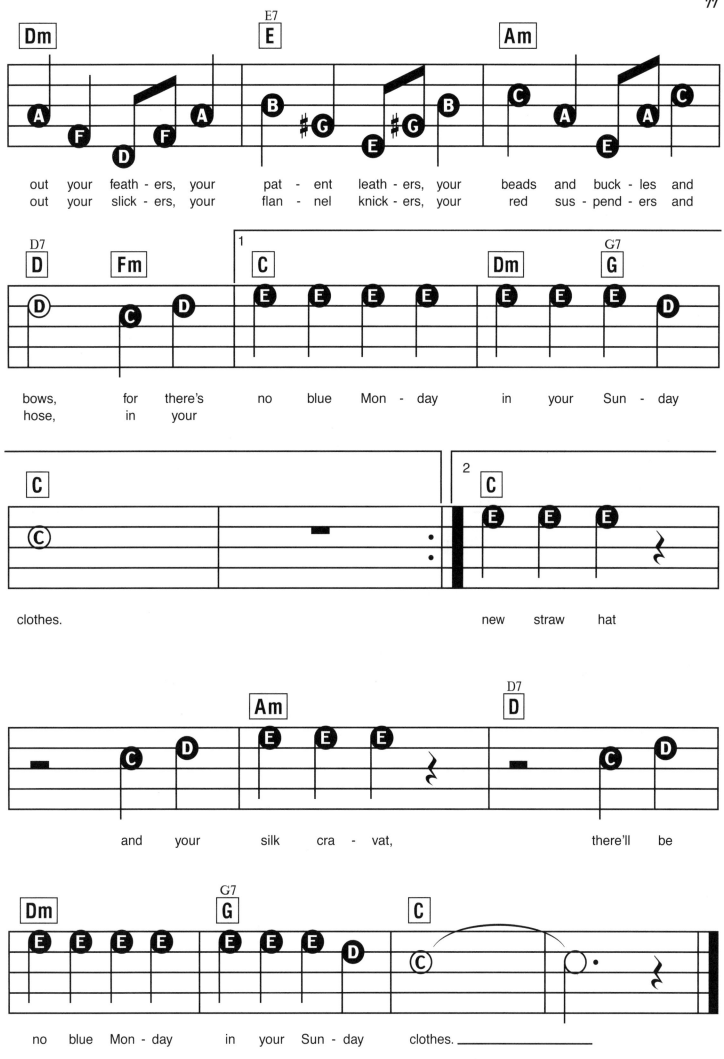

Shall We Dance?
from THE KING AND I

Registration 4
Rhythm: Fox Trot or Swing

Lyrics by Oscar Hammerstein II
Music by Richard Rodgers

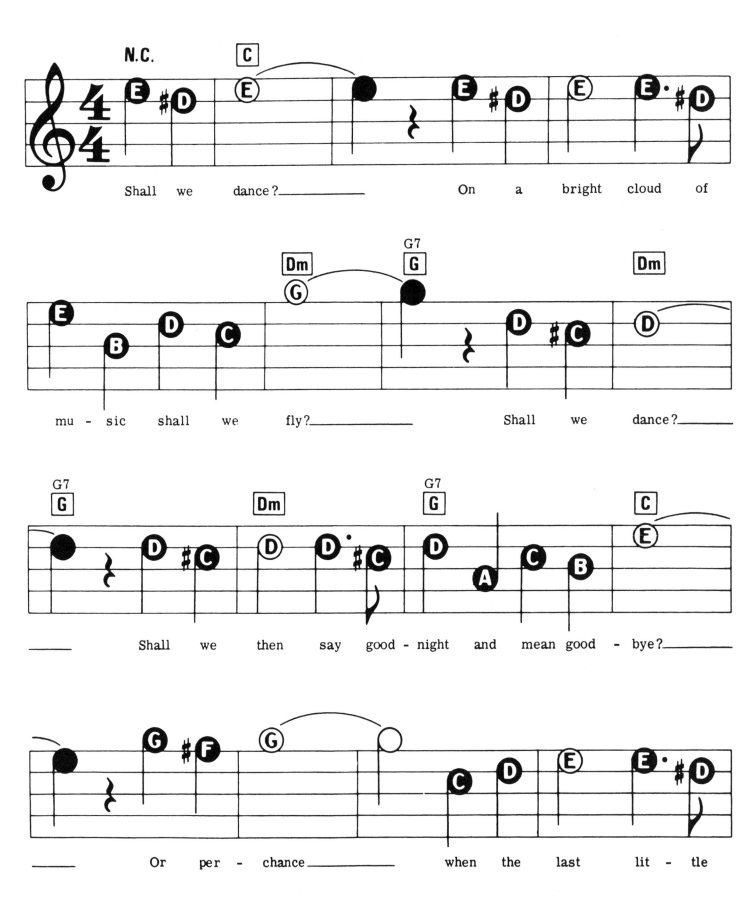

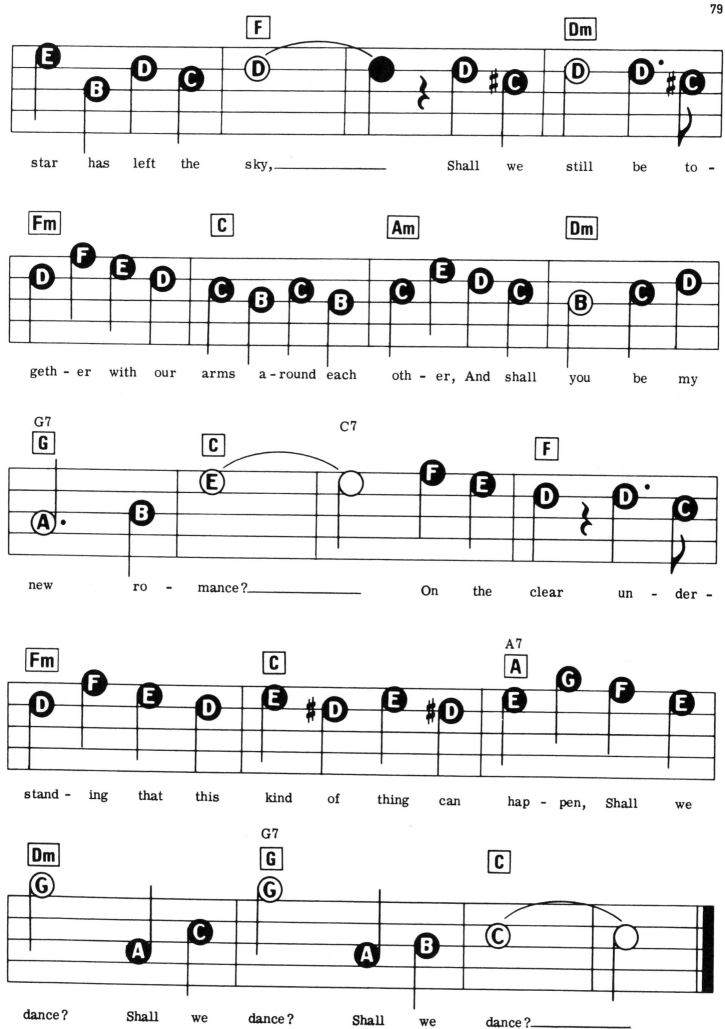

Some Enchanted Evening
from SOUTH PACIFIC

Registration 1
Rhythm: Ballad or Fox Trot

Lyrics by Oscar Hammerstein II
Music by Richard Rodgers

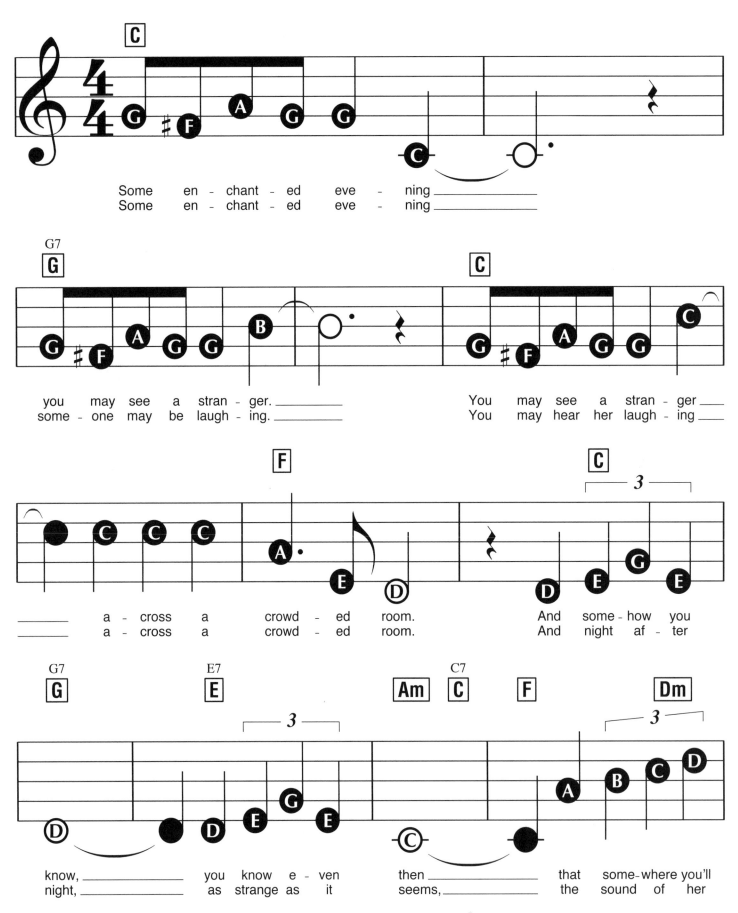

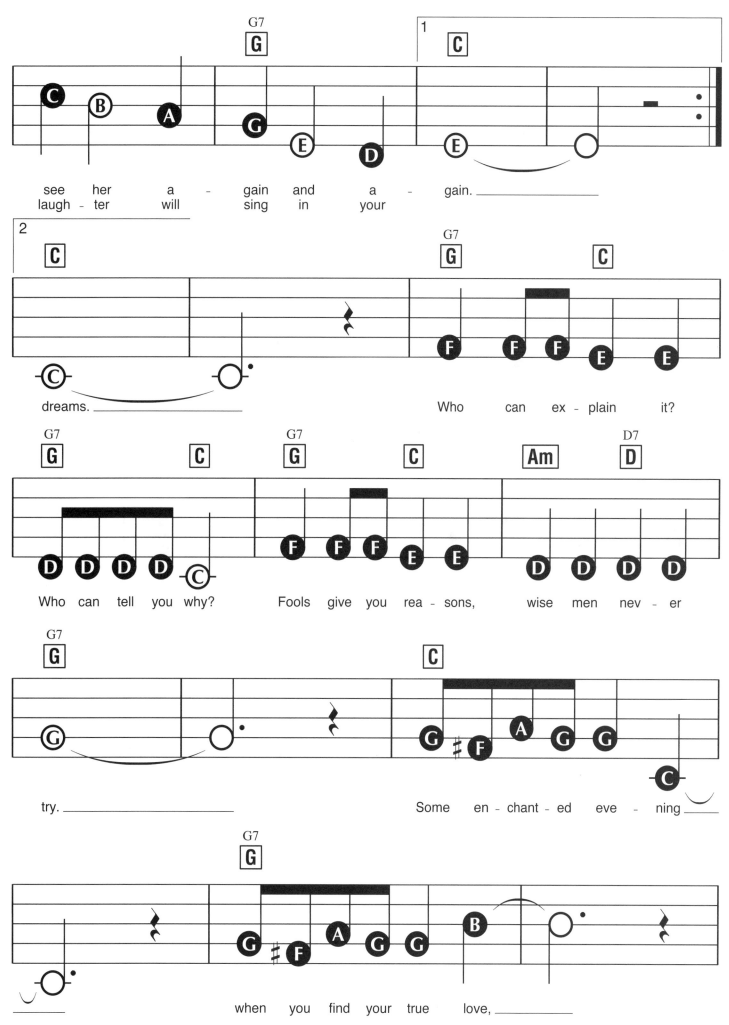

see her a - gain and a - gain. _____

laugh - ter a will sing in your

dreams. _____ Who can ex - plain it?

Who can tell you why? Fools give you rea - sons, wise men nev - er

try. _____ Some en - chant - ed eve - ning _____

when you find your true love, _____

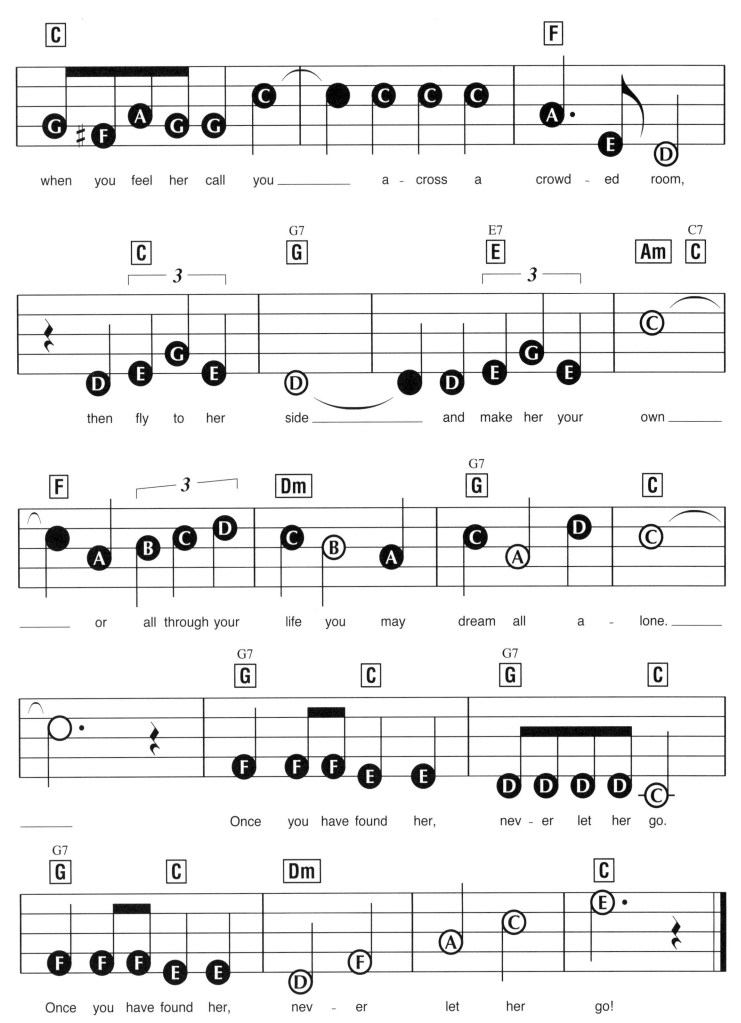

Someone Like You
from the Broadway Musical JEKYLL & HYDE

Registration 3
Rhythm: Ballad

Words and Music by Leslie Bricusse
and Frank Wildhorn

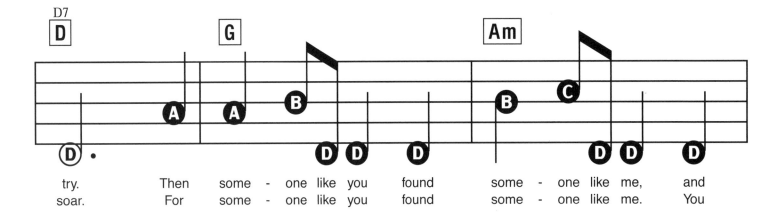

try. Then some - one like you found some - one like me, and
soar. For some - one like you found some - one like me. You

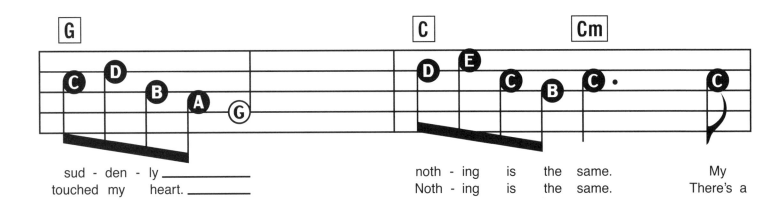

sud - den - ly _____ noth - ing is the same. My
touched my heart. _____ Noth - ing is the same. There's a

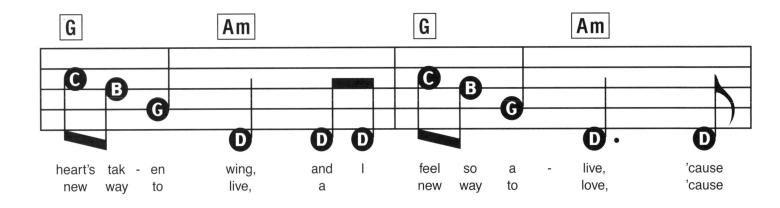

heart's tak - en wing, and I feel so a - live, 'cause
new way to live, a new way to love, 'cause

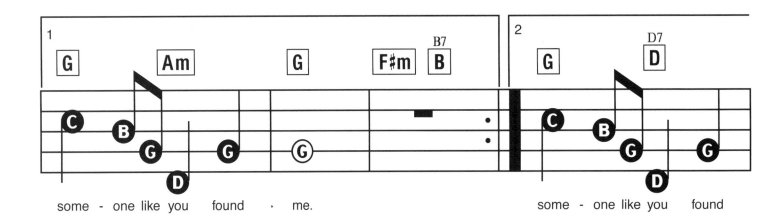

1
some - one like you found me.

2
some - one like you found

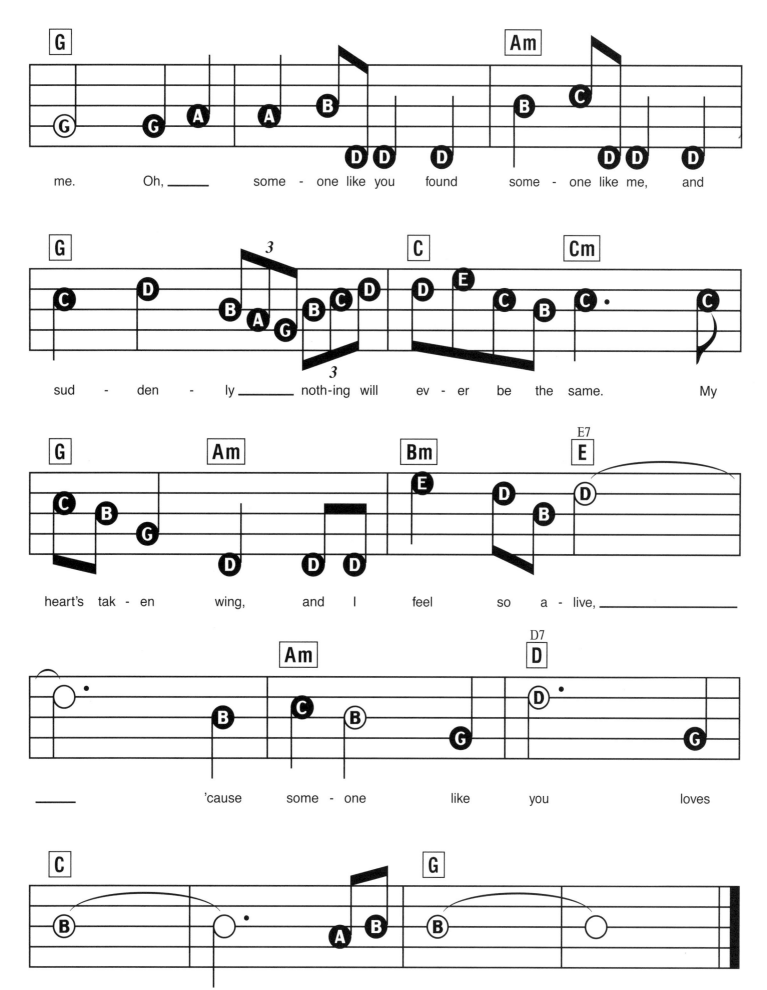

The Sound of Music
from THE SOUND OF MUSIC

Registration 3
Rhythm: Fox Trot or Ballad

Lyrics by Oscar Hammerstein II
Music by Richard Rodgers

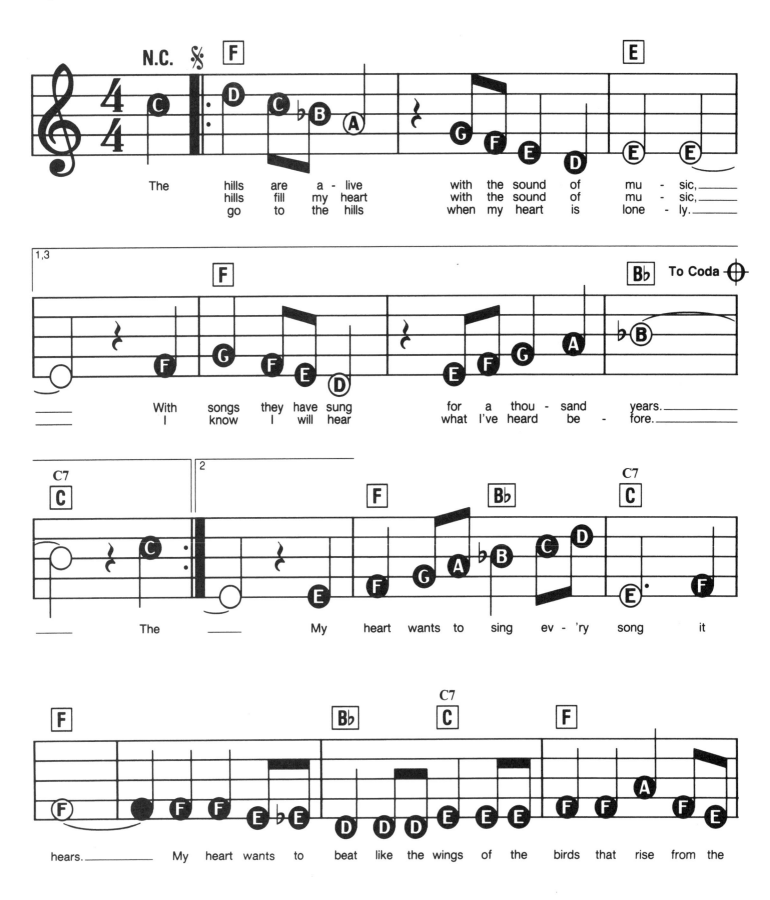

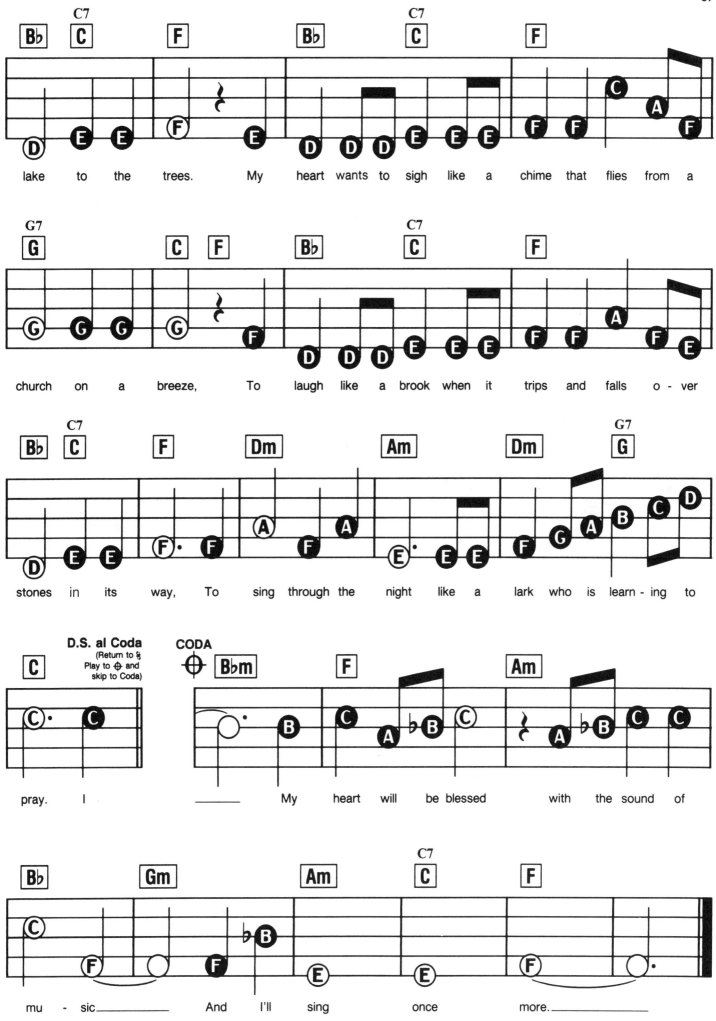

The Surrey with the Fringe on Top
from OKLAHOMA!

Registration 7
Rhythm: Swing

Lyrics by Oscar Hammerstein II
Music by Richard Rodgers

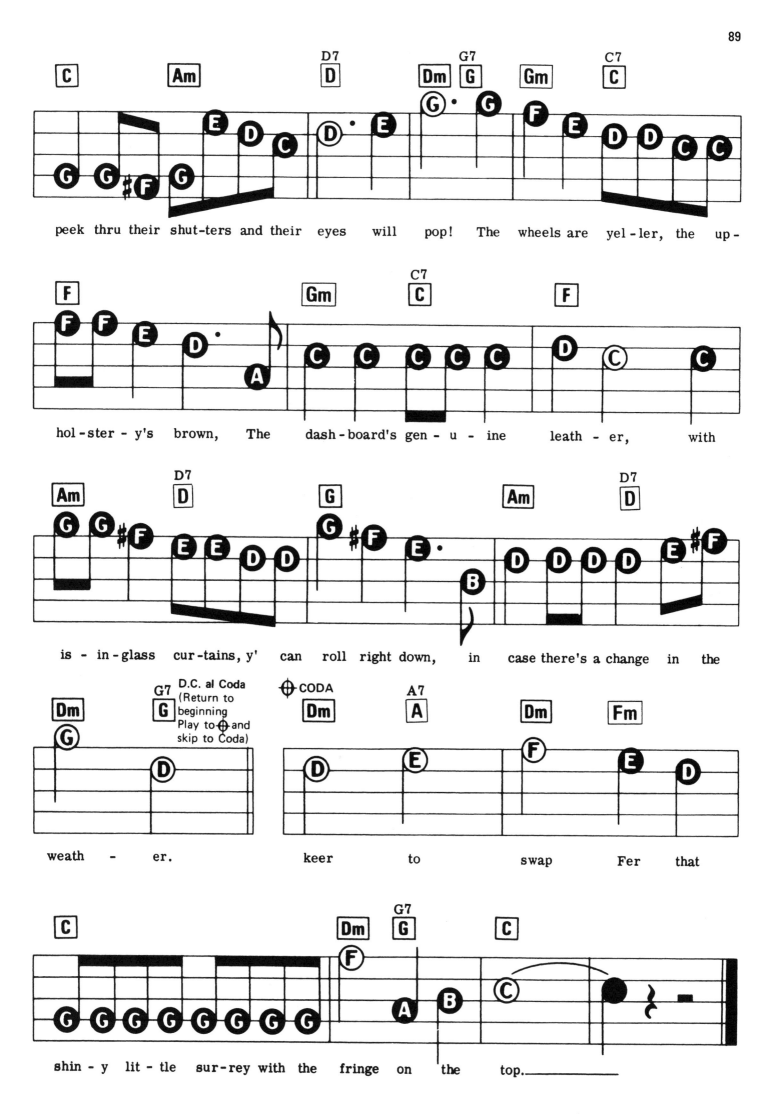

Till There Was You
from Meredith Willson's THE MUSIC MAN

Registration 2
Rhythm: Ballad

By Meredith Willson

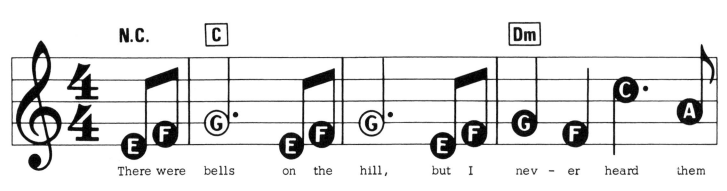

There were bells on the hill, but I nev - er heard them

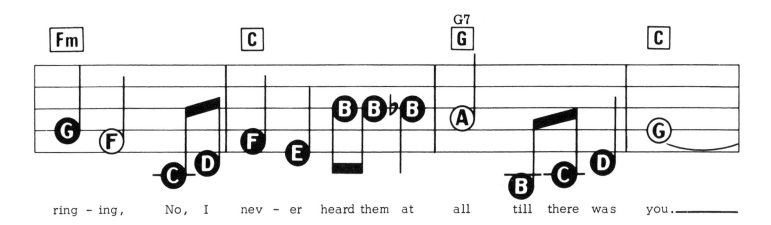

ring - ing, No, I nev - er heard them at all till there was you.

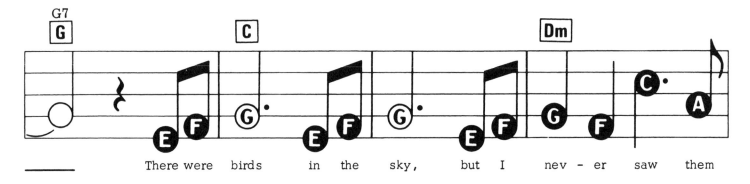

There were birds in the sky, but I nev - er saw them

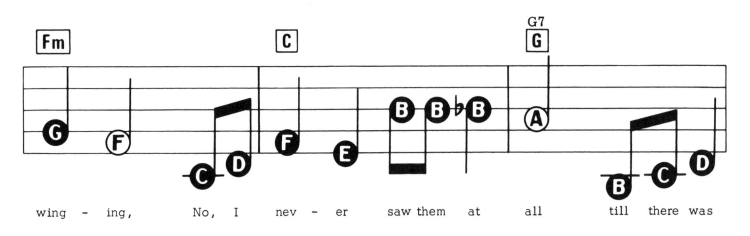

wing - ing, No, I nev - er saw them at all till there was

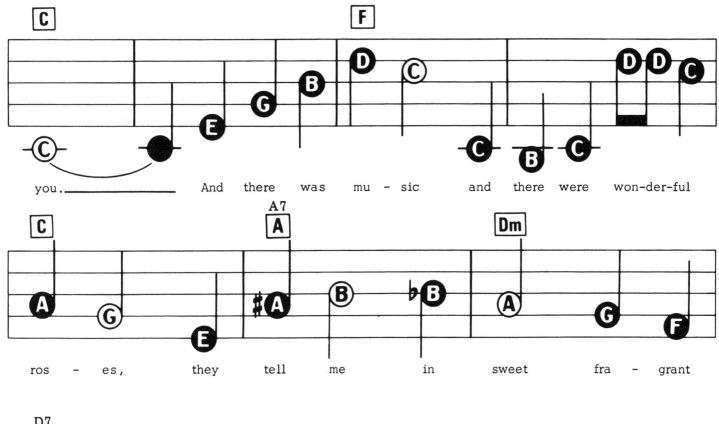

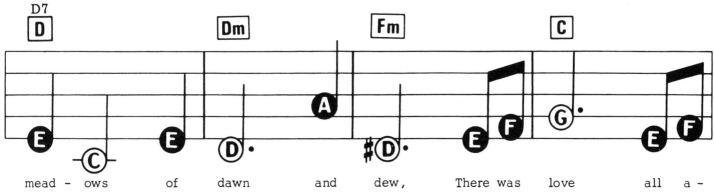

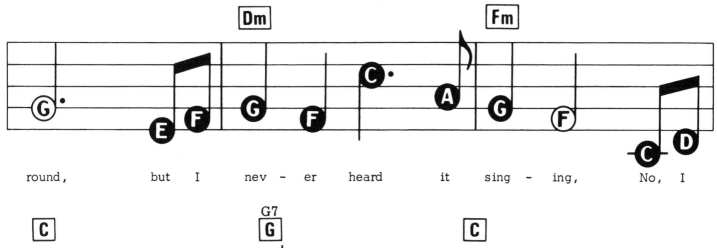

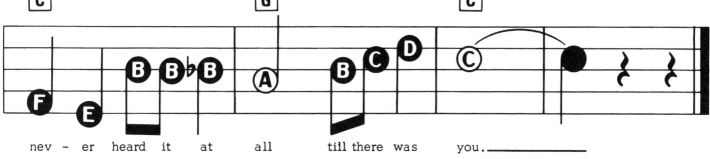

Try to Remember
from THE FANTASTICKS

Registration 8
Rhythm: Waltz

Words by Tom Jones
Music by Harvey Schmidt

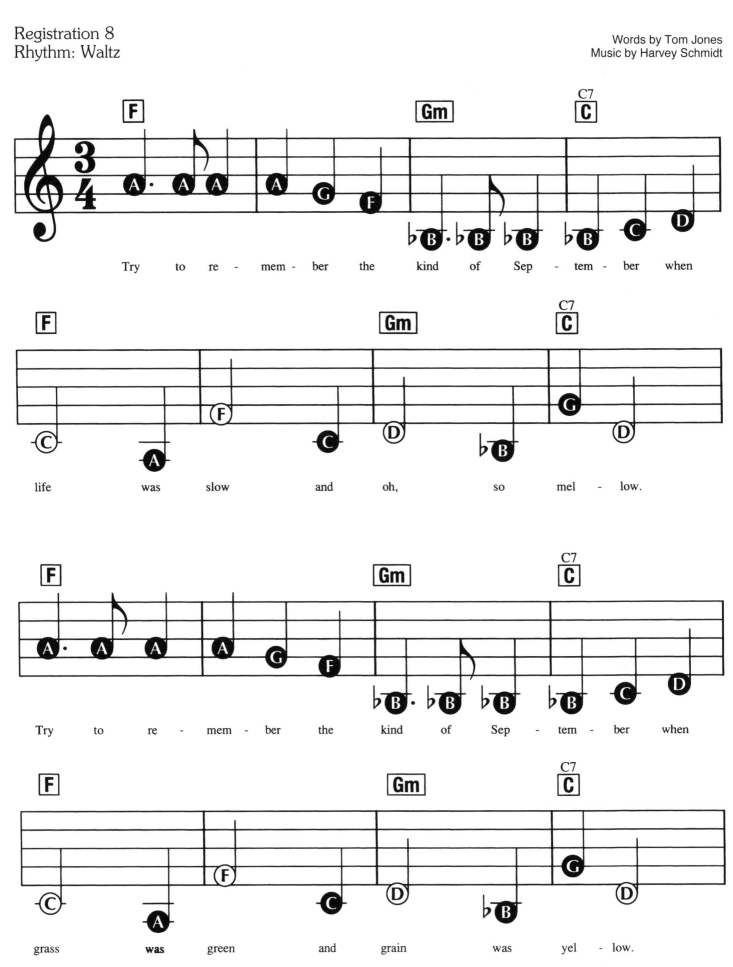

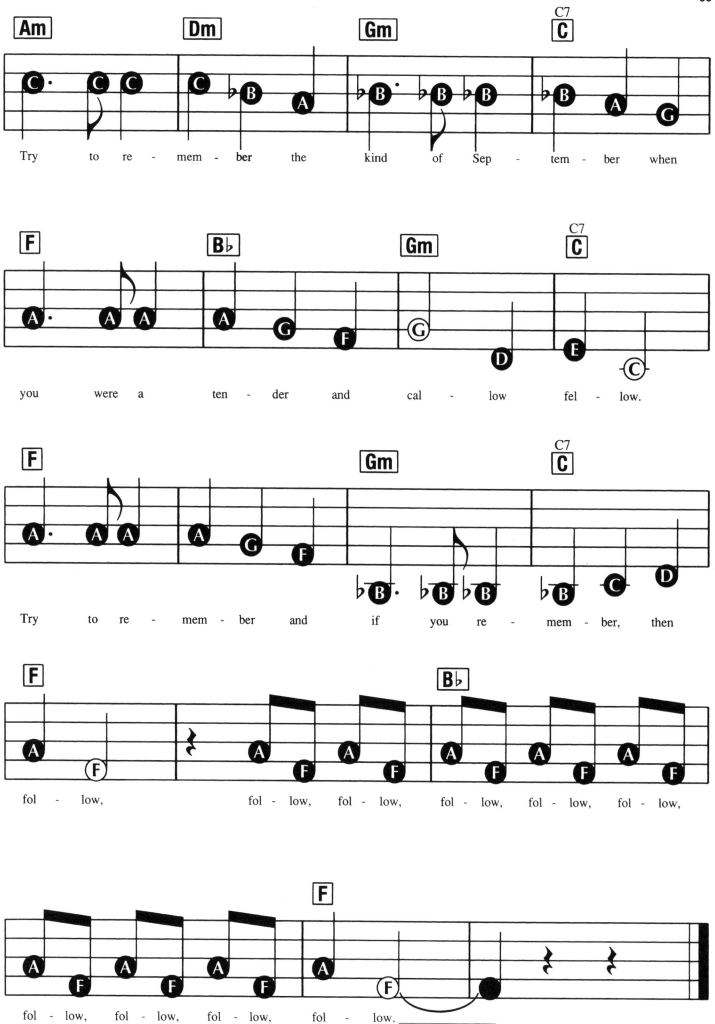

Waving Through a Window
from DEAR EVAN HANSEN

Registration 8
Rhythm: Broadway

Music and Words by Benj Pasek
and Justin Paul

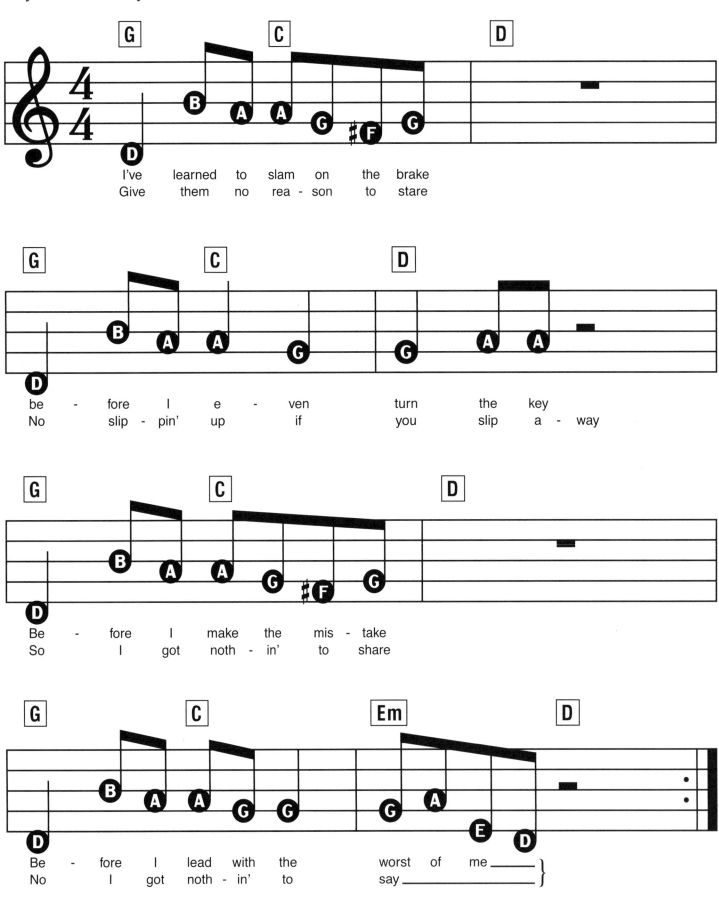

I've learned to slam on the brake
Give them no rea - son to stare

be - fore I e - ven turn the key
No slip - pin' up if you slip a - way

Be - fore I make the mis - take
So I got noth - in' to share

Be - fore I lead with the worst of me ____ }
No I got noth - in' to say _____ }

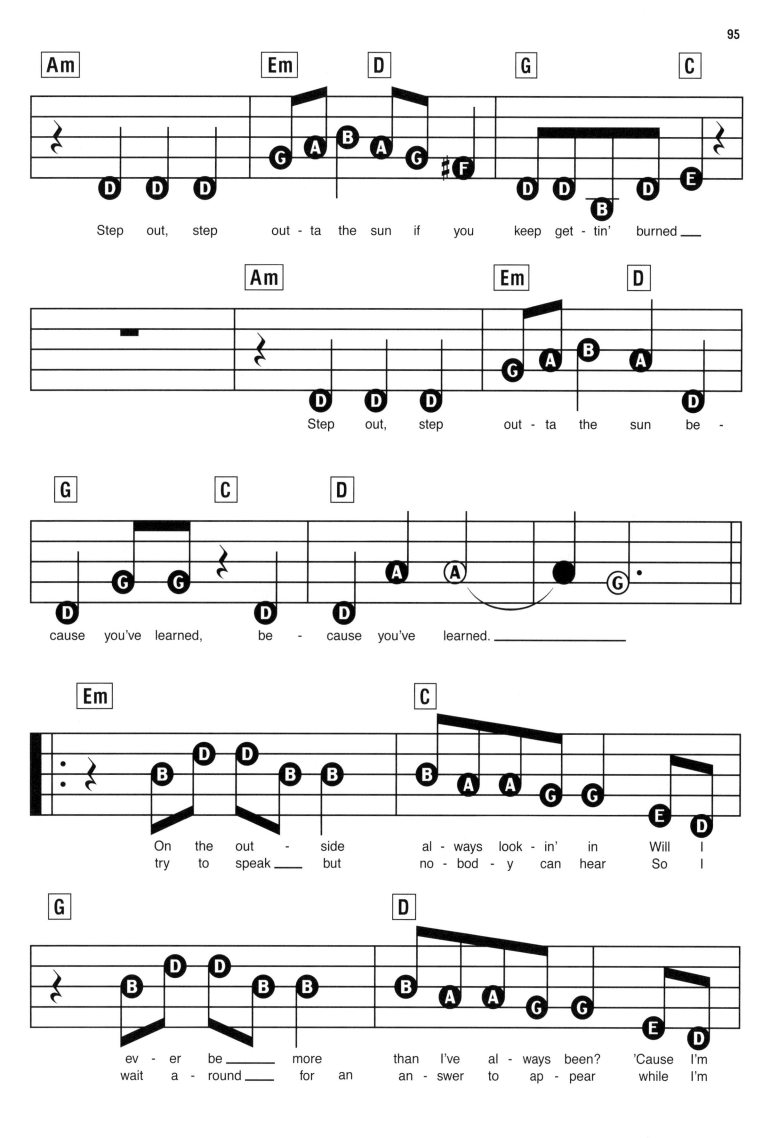

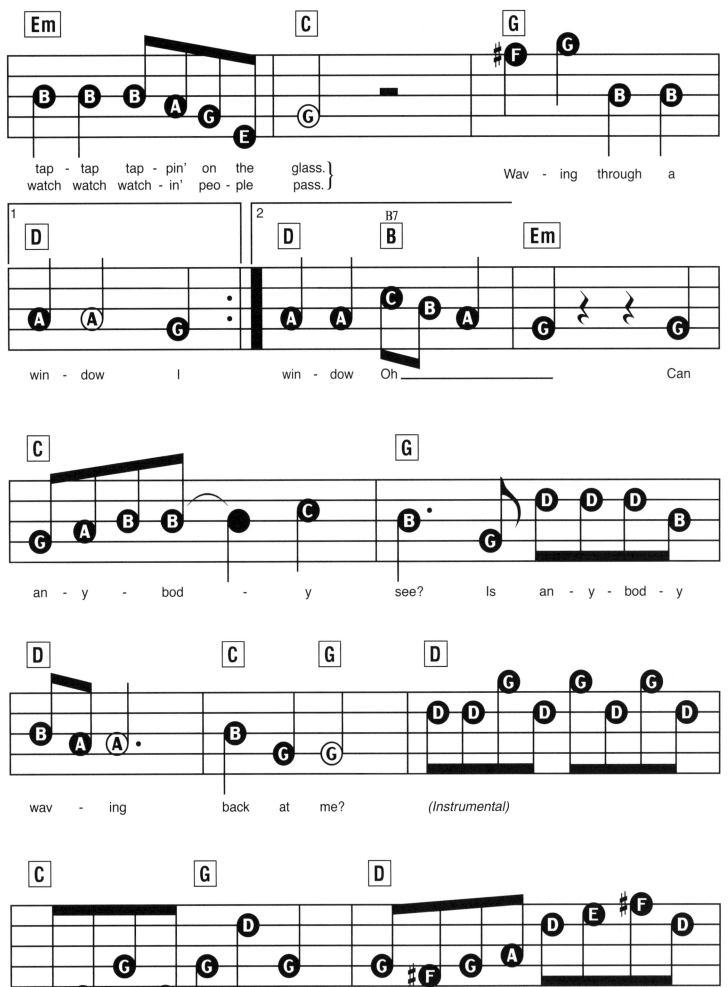

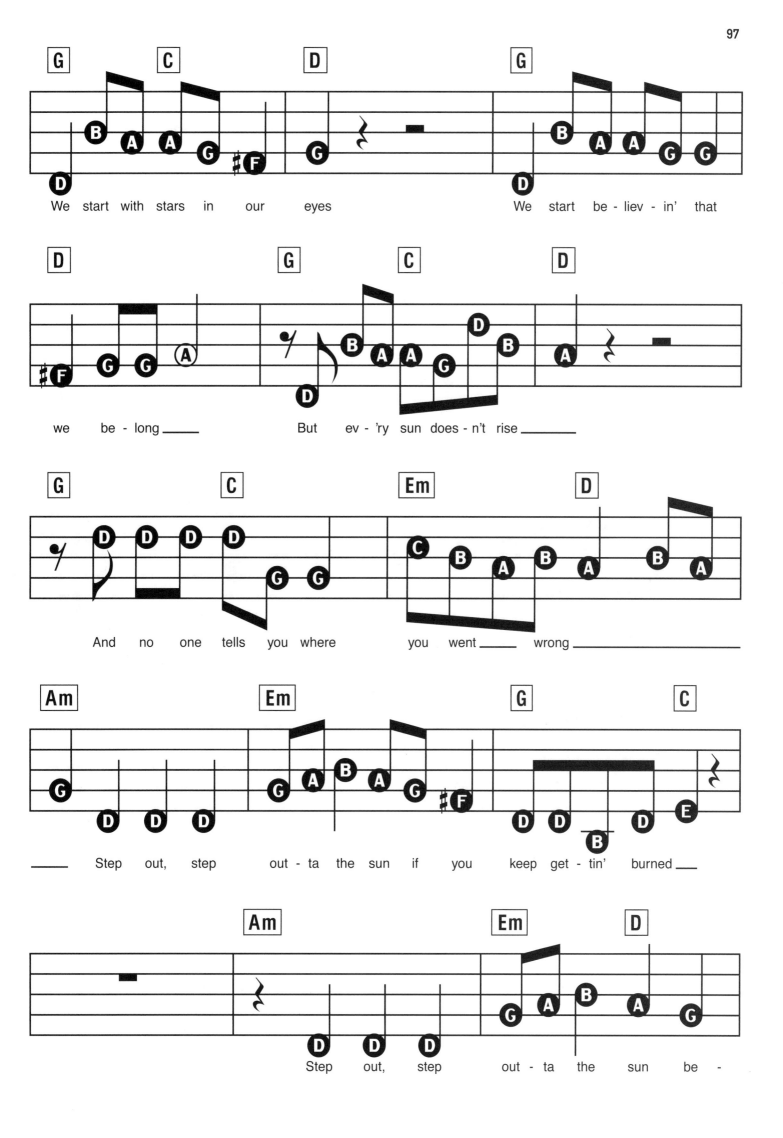

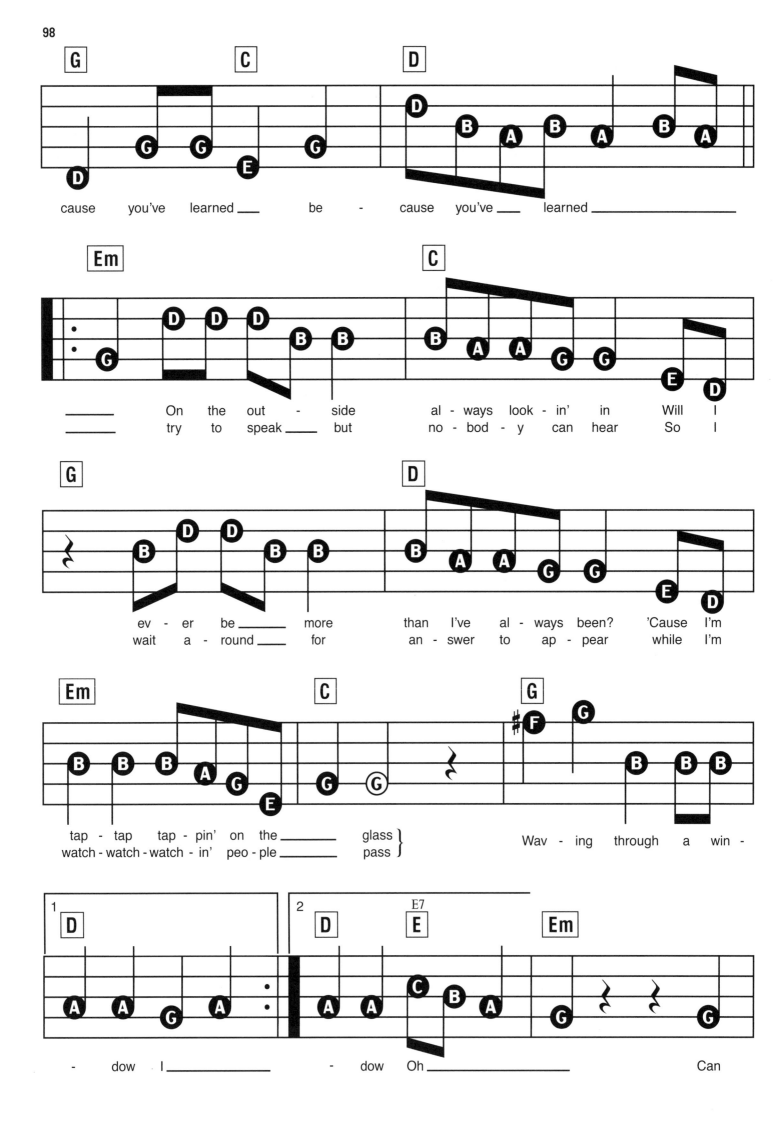

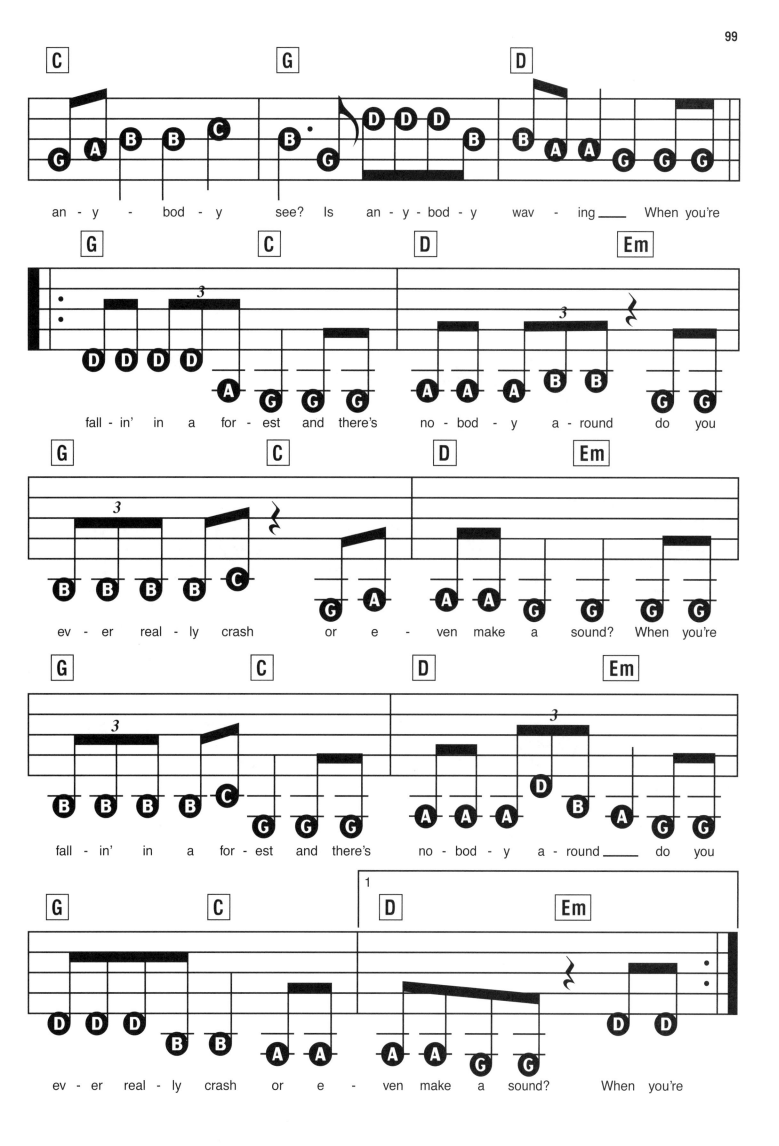

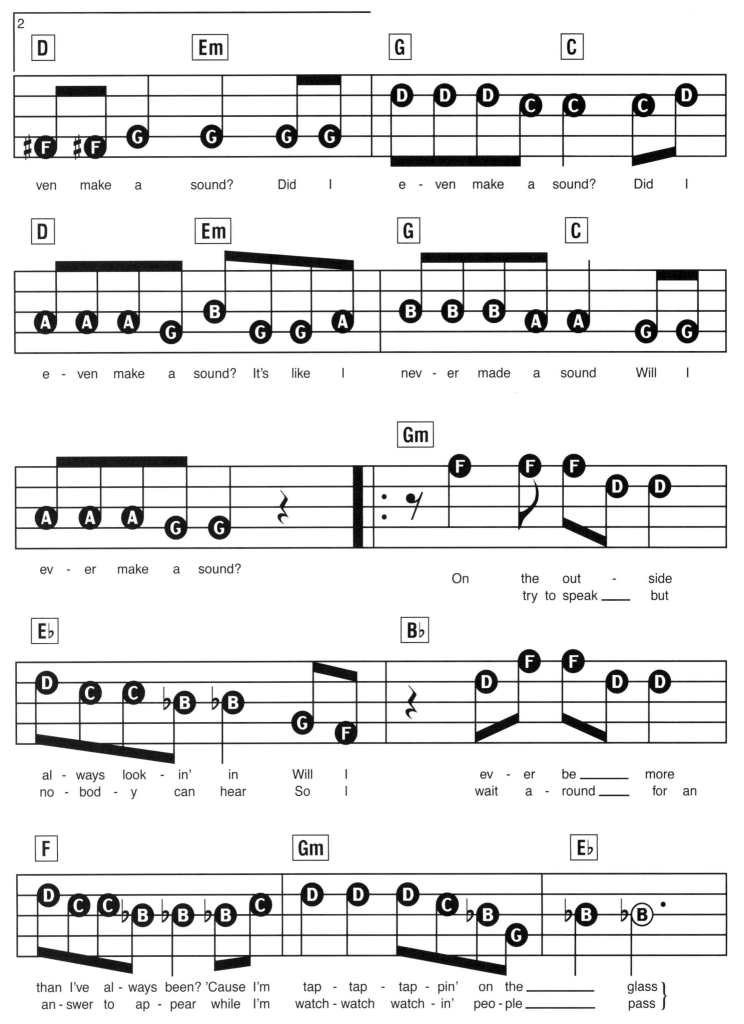

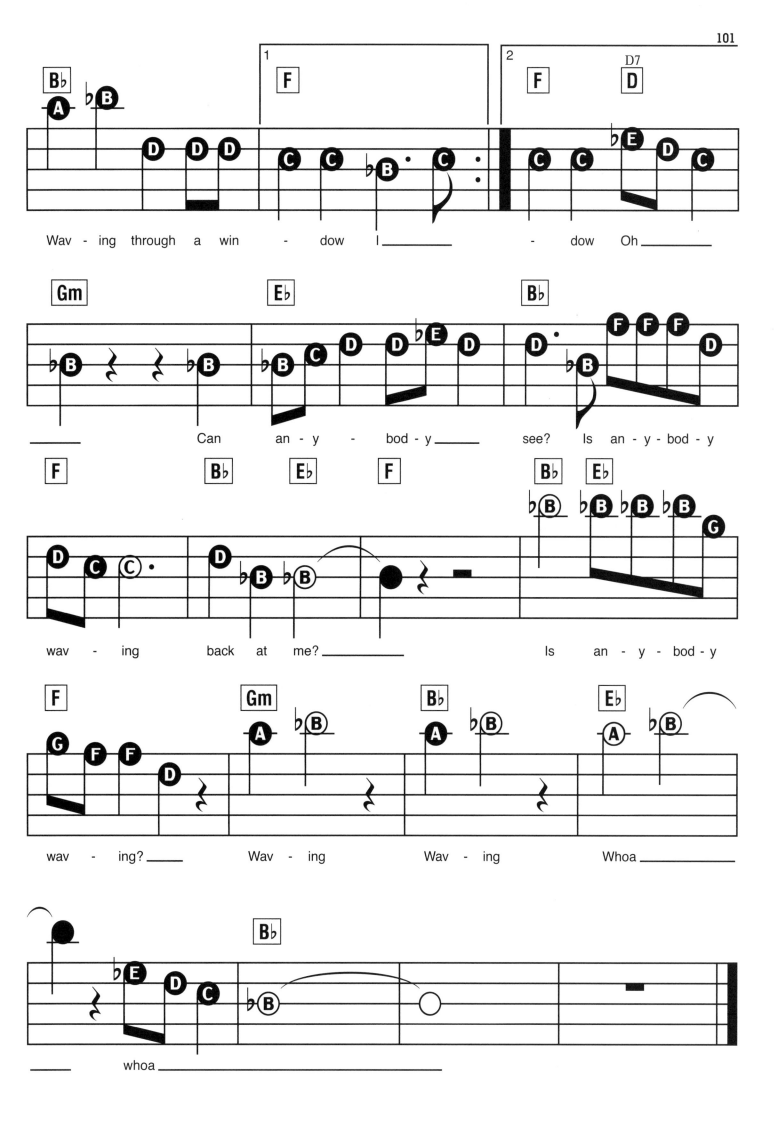

Younger Than Springtime
from SOUTH PACIFIC

Registration 4
Rhythm: Fox Trot or Swing

Lyrics by Oscar Hammerstein II
Music by Richard Rodgers

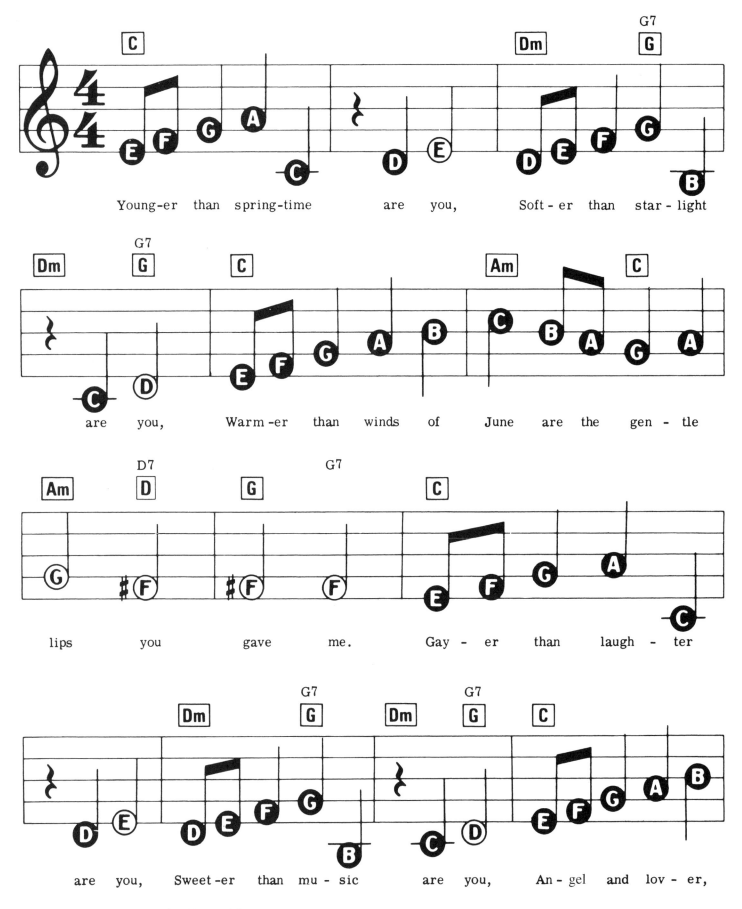

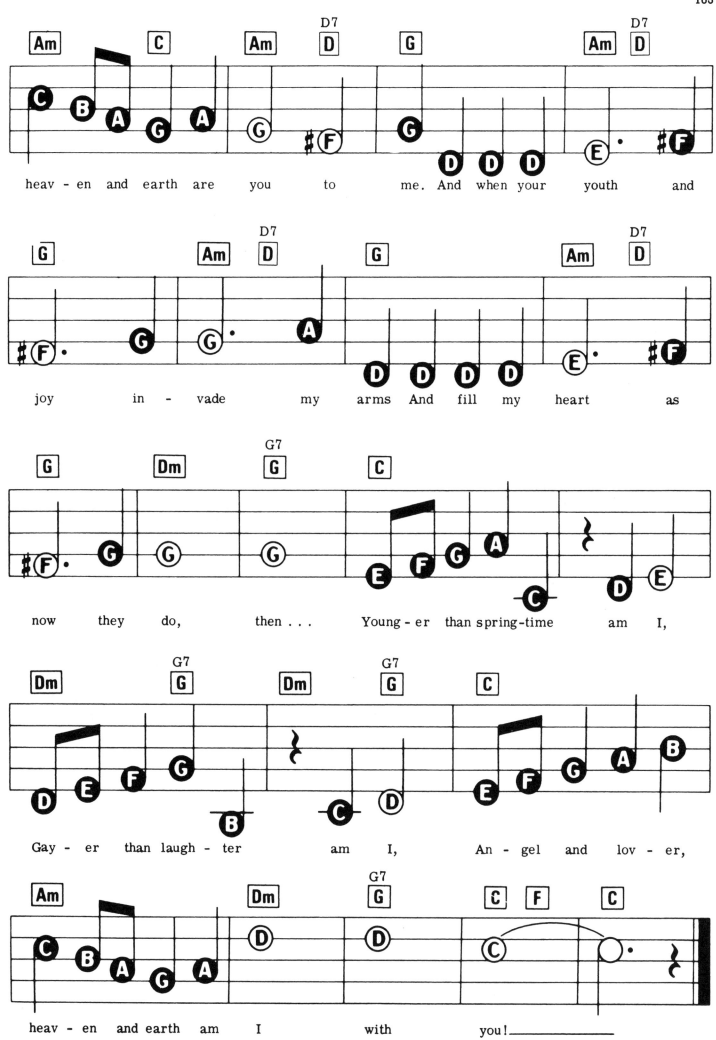

Time Warp
from THE ROCKY HORROR PICTURE SHOW

Registration 2
Rhythm: Rock 'n' Roll or Rock

Words and Music by
Richard O'Brien

N.C. **G** **A**

D E G G G #F G A G E

It's as - tound - ing, time ____ is fleet - ing,

F **C** **G**

F F E C D

mad - ness takes its toll.

D D E G G G G G #F G

But lis - ten close - ly, not for ver - y much

A **F** **C**

A G E F F F E C

long - er. I've got to keep con -

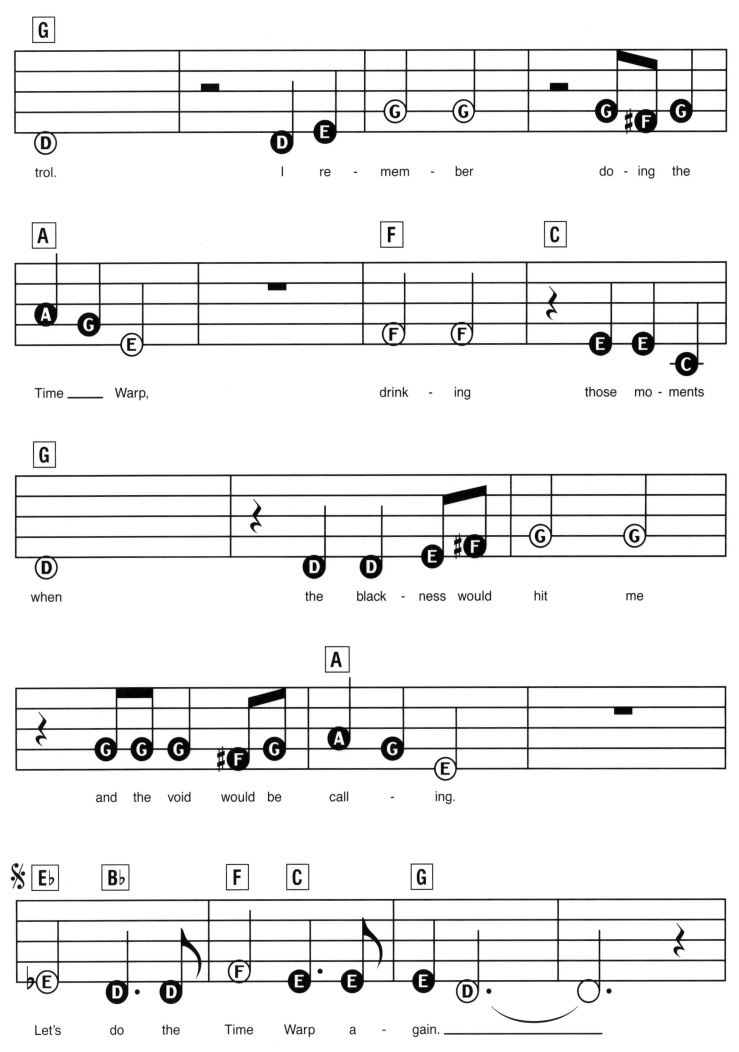

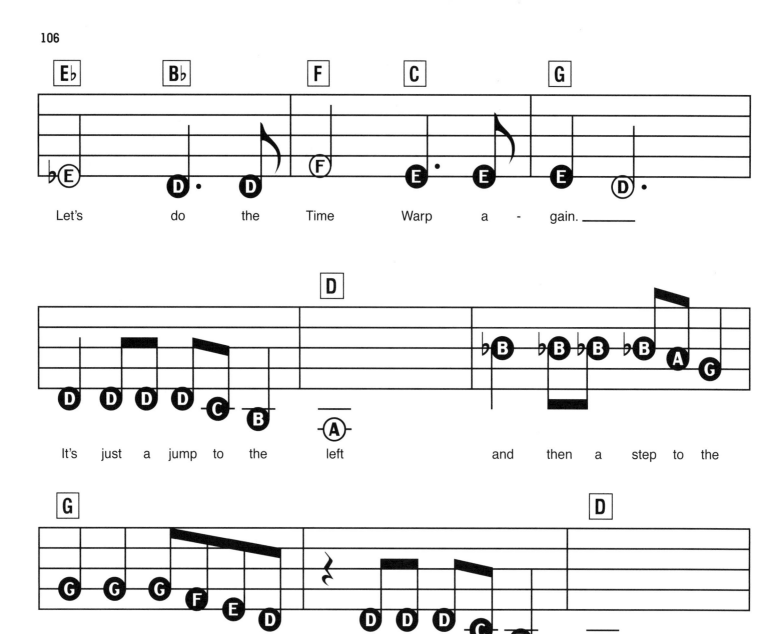

Let's do the Time Warp a - gain. ____

It's just a jump to the left and then a step to the

ri - i - i - i - i - ight. With your hands on your hips,

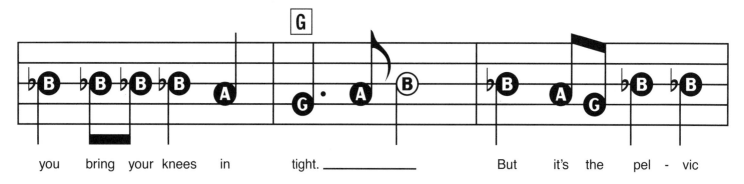

you bring your knees in tight. _____ But it's the pel - vic

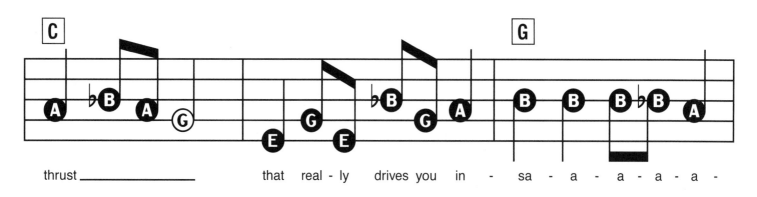

thrust _____ that real - ly drives you in - sa - a - a - a -

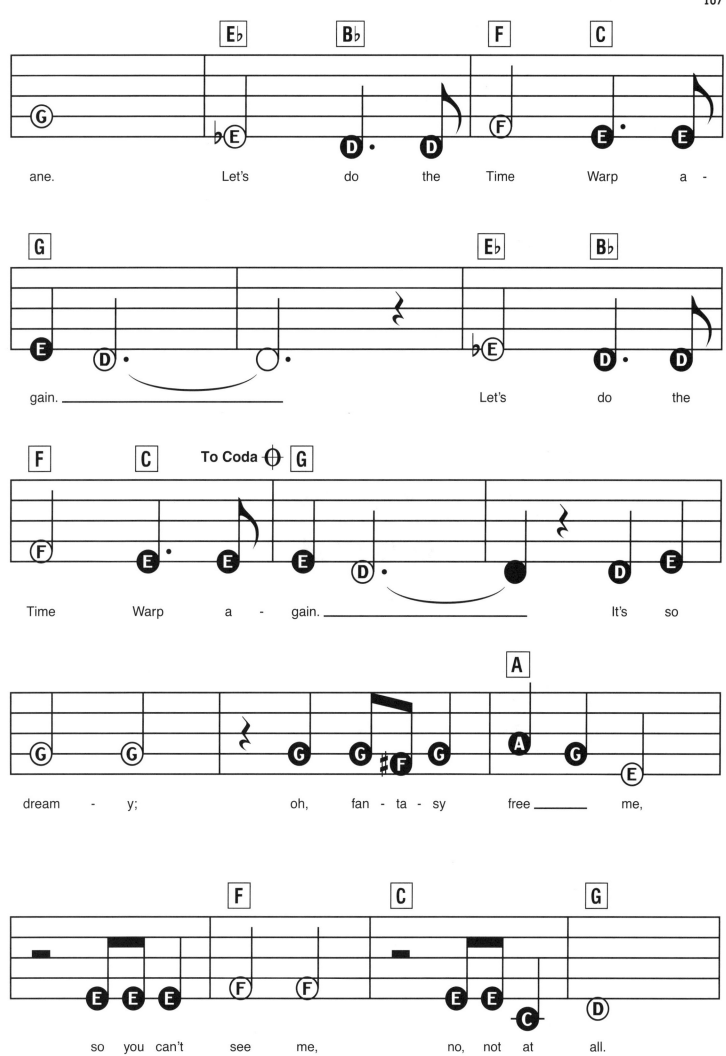

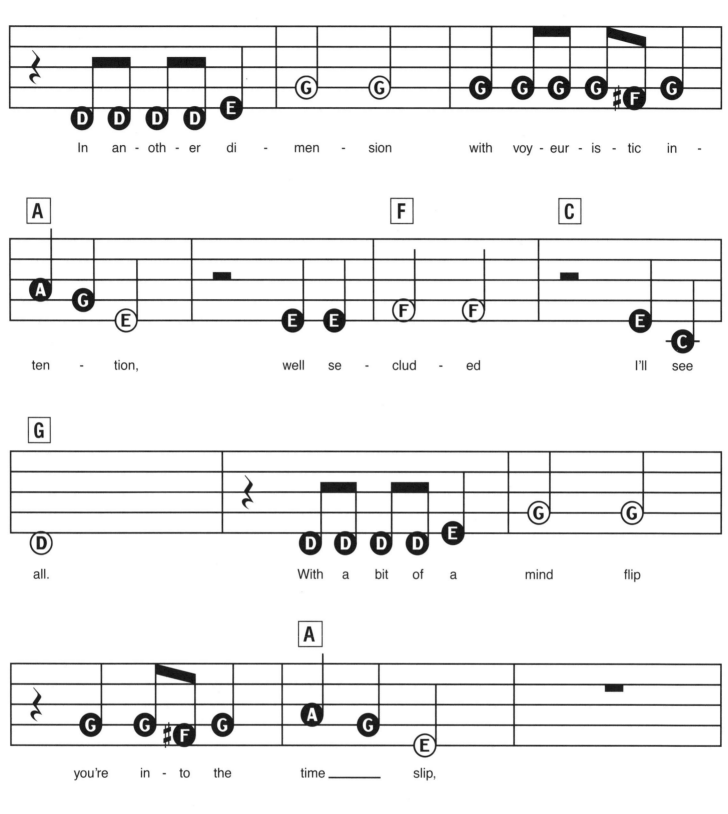

In an - oth - er di - men - sion with voy - eur - is - tic in -

ten - tion, well se - clud - ed I'll see

all. With a bit of a mind flip

you're in - to the time _____ slip,

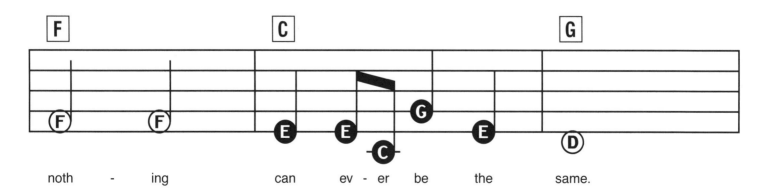

noth - ing can ev - er be the same.

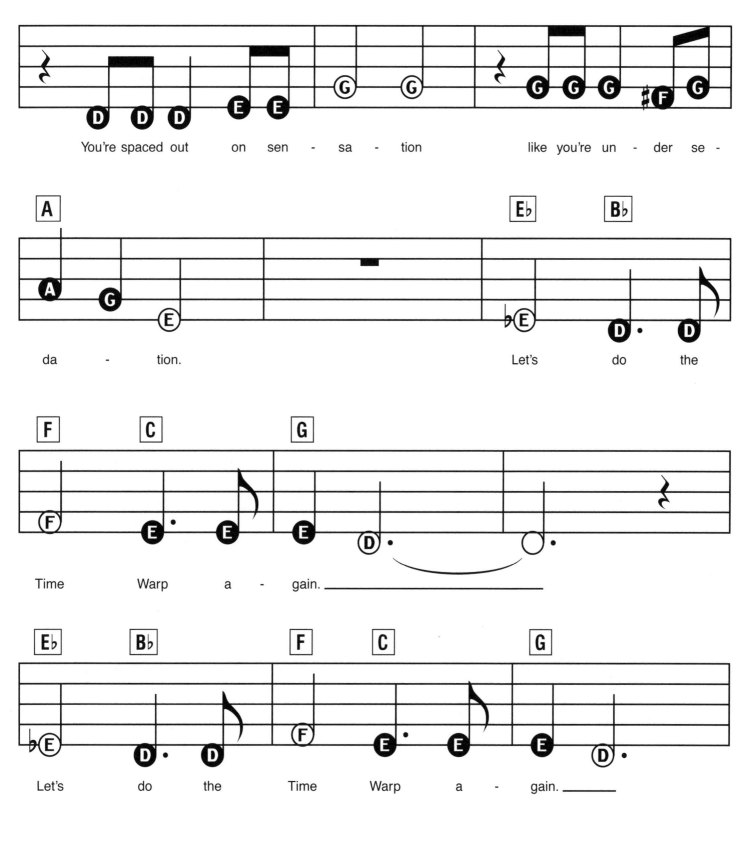

You're spaced out on sen - sa - tion like you're un - der se -

da - tion. Let's do the

Time Warp a - gain. _____

Let's do the Time Warp a - gain. _____

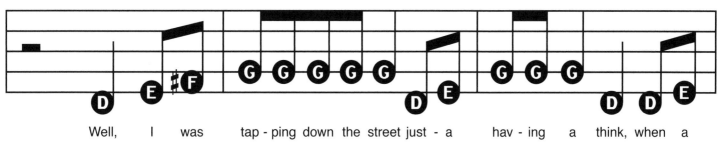

Well, I was tap - ping down the street just - a hav - ing a think, when a

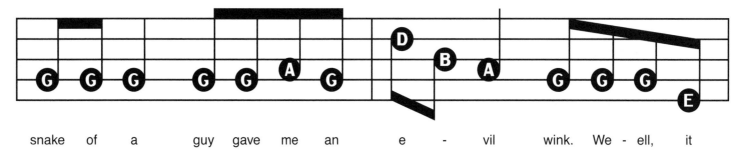

snake of a guy gave me an e - vil wink. We - ell, it

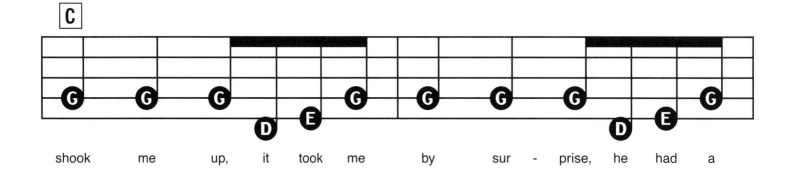

shook me up, it took me by sur - prise, he had a

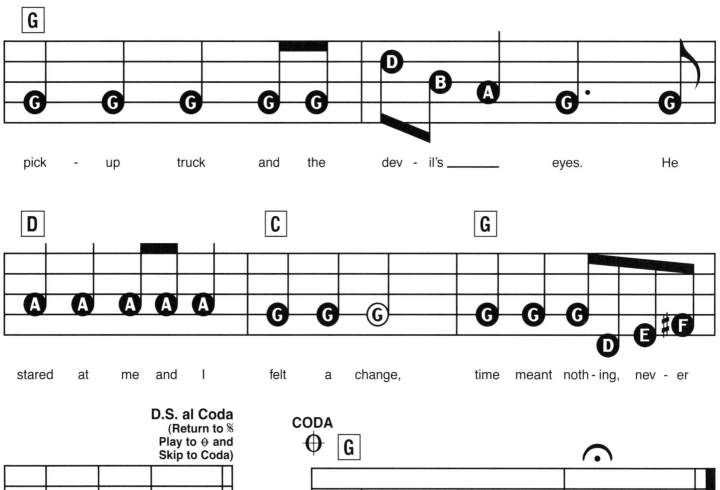

pick - up truck and the dev - il's _____ eyes. He

stared at me and I felt a change, time meant noth - ing, nev - er

D.S. al Coda
(Return to 𝄋
Play to ⊕ and
Skip to Coda)

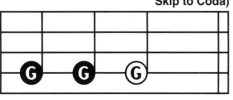

would a - gain.

CODA

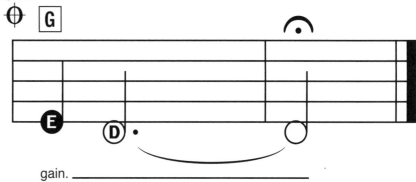

gain. _____

Registration Guide

- Match the Registration number on the song to the corresponding numbered category below. Select and activate an instrumental sound available on your instrument.

- Choose an automatic rhythm appropriate to the mood and style of the song. (Consult your Owner's Guide for proper operation of automatic rhythm features.)

- Adjust the tempo and volume controls to comfortable settings.

Registration

1	Mellow	Flutes, Clarinet, Oboe, Flugel Horn, Trombone, French Horn, Organ Flutes
2	Ensemble	Brass Section, Sax Section, Wind Ensemble, Full Organ, Theater Organ
3	Strings	Violin, Viola, Cello, Fiddle, String Ensemble, Pizzicato, Organ Strings
4	Guitars	Acoustic/Electric Guitars, Banjo, Mandolin, Dulcimer, Ukulele, Hawaiian Guitar
5	Mallets	Vibraphone, Marimba, Xylophone, Steel Drums, Bells, Celesta, Chimes
6	Liturgical	Pipe Organ, Hand Bells, Vocal Ensemble, Choir, Organ Flutes
7	Bright	Saxophones, Trumpet, Mute Trumpet, Synth Leads, Jazz/Gospel Organs
8	Piano	Piano, Electric Piano, Honky Tonk Piano, Harpsichord, Clavi
9	Novelty	Melodic Percussion, Wah Trumpet, Synth, Whistle, Kazoo, Perc. Organ
10	Bellows	Accordion, French Accordion, Mussette, Harmonica, Pump Organ, Bagpipes

FOR ORGANS, PIANOS & ELECTRONIC KEYBOARDS

E-Z PLAY® TODAY PUBLICATION

The E-Z Play® Today songbook series is the shortest distance between beginning musi
playing fun! Check out this list of highlights and visit www.halleonard.com for a com
listing of all volumes and songlists.

HAL•LEONAR

Prices, contents, and availability subject to change without